WRITERS AND THEIR WORK

ISOBEL ARMSTRONG
General Editor

CAROL ANN DUFFY

CAROL ANN DUFFY

Deryn Rees-Jones

Third Edition

© Copyright 1999, 2001 and 2010 by Deryn Rees-Jones

First published in 1999
Second edition 2001
Third edition 2010 published by Northcote House Publishers Ltd,
Horndon House, Horndon, Tavistock, Devon, United Kingdom, PL19 9NQ
Tel: +44 (0) 1822 810066 Fax: +44 (0) 1822 810034

British Library Cataloguing-in-Publication Data
A catalogue record for this book is available from the British Library

ISBN 978-0-7463-1199-8

Typeset by PDQ Typesetting, Newcastle-under-Lyme
Printed and bound in the United Kingdom

for my mother

Contents

Acknowledgements

Thanks to Isobel Armstrong for her invaluable help and enthusiasm, particularly when confronted with the processes of collage; to Alice Harker at Anvil Press, and Gladys Mary Coles at Headland for their friendly advice and prompt replies; and especially to Matt Simpson, Alison Mark and Michael Murphy for all their encouragement and suggestions.

Thanks to Anvil for permission to quote from 'The Dummy', 'Standing Female Nude', 'Mean Time' and 'Mrs Tiresias'; and from 'Oppenheim's Cup and Saucer', 'Translation', 'Girlfriends', 'Homesick' and 'Prayer' in full; and to Picador for permission to quote 'Demeter'.

Thanks also to Carol Ann Duffy for taking the time to look over an earlier draft and for making factual corrections; also for permission to quote the poems 'Dream' and 'Fifth Last Song' which appeared in her Headland collection *Fifth Last Song* (1982); and 'Twins', which was first published in the *Sunday Times*.

Thanks are due also to Liverpool Hope University College who awarded me the fellowship which gave me the time to complete this book.

Biographical Outline

1955	Born Glasgow 23 December. While still a child, her family moves to Staffordshire where she is educated first at a convent school and then at a girls' grammar school.
1973	Her first pamphlet of poems *Fleshweathercock*, written during her teens, is published by Howard Sergeant's Outposts Press.
1977	Graduates from the University of Liverpool with a degree in Philosophy, and in the same year *Beauty and the Beast*, a small pamphlet of work by Duffy and Adrian Henri, appears.
1981	Moves to London.
1982	A pamphlet of poems, *Fifth Last Song*, is published, and a two-act play, *Take My Husband*, is performed at the Liverpool Playhouse.
1982–4	Holds a C. Day Lewis Fellowship, working as a writer in East London schools.
1983	Wins first prize in the National Poetry Competition, and also receives a Scottish Arts Council Award. Publishes another small pamphlet, *Thrown Voices* (Turret). Poetry Editor, *Ambit* magazine.
1984	*Cavern of Dreams* performed. Receives an Eric Gregory Award from the Society of Authors for poets under the age of 30.
1985	*Standing Female Nude*, her first full-length adult collection, is published by Anvil. It receives excellent reviews.
1986	Continues to write both poetry and drama. Her play *Loss* is broadcast on BBC radio in July and *Little Women, Big Boys* is performed at the Almeida, London.
1987	Duffy's second collection, *Selling Manhattan*, is pub-

lished, again by Anvil.

1988   Receives a Somerset Maugham Award from the Society of Authors, the purpose of which is to enable her to travel.

1989   Receives a Dylan Thomas Award for her third collection with Anvil, *The Other Country*, which wins another Scottish Arts Council Book Award.

1992   A small pamphlet, *William and the Ex-Prime Minister*, appears. She wins a Cholmondeley Award.

1993   Fourth collection with Anvil, *Mean Time*, wins a Forward Prize, Scottish Arts Council Book Award, and the Whitbread Award for poetry.

1994   *Selected Poems* published by Penguin. Works with Tim Supple at the Young Vic on stage adaptations of Grimm, published by Faber as *Grimm Tales* (1996) and *More Grimm Tales* (1997).

1995   Birth of daughter, Ella. Receives the prestigious Lannan Literary Award in the United States. Awarded the OBE.

1996   Moves from London to Manchester. Lectures part-time at Manchester Metropolitan University.

1998   A selection of recent poems, *The Pamphlet*, is published by Anvil.

1999   Becomes a favourite for the post of poet laureate after the death of Ted Hughes. *The World's Wife* shortlisted for the Forward Prize. *Meeting Midnight* shortlisted for the Whitbread Children's Book of the Year.

             Robert W. Woodruff Library, Atlanta, Georgia, buys literary papers; Duffy made Fellow of the Royal Society of Letters.

2000   Death of close friend, Adrian Henri.

2001   Receives £75,000 award from Nesta (National Endowment for Science, Technology and the Arts) over a period of five years to give her more time for writing, particularly to concentrate on her writing for children. 'I want to dedicate some of my time to writing new poems for children, to bring the same seriousness of intent to these poems as I bring to my work for adults. Hopefully, I can open doors to the

	imagination where children can write for them-
	selves.' She is awarded the CBE.
2002	Publishes *Feminine Gospels* with Picador.
2004	Edits anthology *Out of Fashion* (Picador). Premier of production *Beasts and Beauties,* with Tim Supple at Bristol Old Vic. *New Selected Poems* (Picador) published.
2005	Publishes *Rapture* (Picador), which charts a new relationship, and its unhappy end. Also publishes *Moon Zoo,* a poetry collection for children, and *Another Night Before Christmas,* a retelling of Victorian poet Clement Moore's children's poem 'A Night Before Christmas' (John Murray).
2006	Wins T.S. Eliot award for poetry for *Rapture. Selected Poems* (Penguin) published. Also publishes a children's tale, *The Lost Happy Endings,* with illustrations by Jane Ray.
2007	Edits anthology: *Answering Back: Living Poets Reply to the Poetry of the Past* (Picador); premier of play *Casanova* at Lyric Theatre Hammersmith; premier of *The Manchester Carols* at the Royal Northern College of Music, written with music by composer and soprano Sasha Johnson Manning. The sixteen carols retell the Christmas story for the 21st century.
2008	Publishes collection of children's poems *The Hat* (Faber).
2009	Appointed Poet Laureate.

Abbreviations and References

I have used the *Selected Poems* (Harmondsworth: Penguin, 1994) where possible, cited in the text as *SP*, followed by a page number. The following abbreviations have been used in citing other poems from Duffy's individual collections, or from selections of her poems:

FLS   *Fifth Last Song* (Liverpool: Headland, 1982)
MT   *Mean Time* (London: Anvil, 1993)
PMP   *Penguin Modern Poets* 2 (Harmondsworth: Penguin, 1995)
SFN   *Standing Female Nude* (London: Anvil, 1985)
SM   *Selling Manhattan* (London: Anvil, 1987)
TOC   *The Other Country* (London: Anvil, 1990)
WW   *The World's Wife* (London: Picador, 1999)

Prologue

Carol Ann Duffy has influenced a whole generation of poets writing or beginning to write in the 1980s, and brought an eclectic range of influences to bear on the contemporary poetry scene. Her contribution also reflects the beginnings of a change that has recently taken place in British poetry. This change is remarked on by the editors of Bloodaxe's *The New Poetry* as one that brings

> accessibility, democracy and responsiveness, humour and serious-ness, and reaffirms the art's significance as public utterance.... It is fresh in its attitudes, risk-taking in its address, and plural in its forms and voices.[1]

It might be argued that Duffy is one of the key factors in this change. Her attempts to strip bare the linguistic devices of poetic language, and to explore some of the patterns and rhythms of everyday, non-standard English, have made her accessible to a wide readership. The snappy sentences, and apparent simplicity of her work, however, do not prevent Duffy from addressing complex philosophical issues about the function of language and the construction of the self, or from dealing with a wide range of issues, from the effects of sexism, racism, immigration, domestic violence, and social disaffection, to the complexities of love.

Although a non-British tradition, which includes the work of the French poet Jacques Prévert (1900–77), the Chilean poet Pablo Neruda (1904–73) and the black French-speaking poet from Martinique, Aimé Césaire (b. 1913), has been of obvious importance to Duffy, she can also, perhaps not surprisingly, be read as very much a part of a tradition of British poetry. We can trace the influence of Wordsworth (her interest in childhood and memory, and her desire to speak the language of the 'common man'), of Browning (her use of the monologue) and of Auden (her interest in the vernacular and popular forms). We

1

can see how the nostalgia and disaffection of Philip Larkin blend surprisingly with the surrealism of Dylan Thomas and Ted Hughes; how her interest in language and the monologue corresponds with the interests of the Scottish poet W. S. Graham (1942–77). Importantly, too, we can see how the early influence of Eliot rubs curiously alongside that of the Beats, and the Liverpool poets with whom she associated in the 1970s.

While there is an impulse towards realism running throughout Duffy's work, her early interest in the Romantics and her journey through Modernist and Surrealist practices have culminated in an aesthetic which seeks to problematize notions of truth and the desire to mediate an 'authentic' experience while relentlessly searching for new ways in which to explore and examine them. And it is perhaps this tension – between the Romantic and the Modern, between her impulse, on the one hand to tell it as it is, and her more postmodern sensibilities – which is the key to her poetics.

Duffy's work marks a transition between a mainstream and a more experimental aesthetic. But it may also be seen as a bridge between a feminist and postfeminist *poetics*, forging as it does a link between those women writing directly out of experiences of feminism and the burgeoning of the second wave of the Women's Movement in the 1970s, and those in the 1990s who, while still not holding an unproblematic position with the poetic tradition, have benefited from twenty years of feminist activity and radical changes in their position within society – political, sexual and economic.

Although, in the 1970s, the Women's Movement was able to foster and, to some extent, legitimize women's experiences, and to validate a desire for self-expression, much of the poetry which arose directly from feminist activity was still very much outside the mainstream; its necessarily urgent and explicit political agenda was seen as limiting its status as art. In 1988, Duffy's anxiety about defining herself as a feminist remains evident in her approach to the role of both woman and poet. She explains:

> I don't mind being called a feminist poet, but I wouldn't mind if I wasn't. I think the concerns of art can go beyond that. I think as long as the work is read it doesn't really matter what the cover is. I have never in my life sat down and thought 'I will write a feminist poem'...[2]

2

Duffy's poetic, as we shall see, is one which had to be carefully constructed (whether consciously or unconsciously) in order to countermand a whole range of expectations about women's poetry and women's roles prevalent in the mid-1980s when she was first publishing.

In moving beyond a straightforwardly feminist poetry, Duffy does not, however, forget the importance of women's experience, the difficulties of women's lives, and the difficulties that patriarchy presents to both men and women. Moreover, in her refusal to conform to any stereotypical notion of femininity, feminism or women's poetry, she has opened up many exciting and important possibilities for the range of poetry and for its audience, exploring as she does issues of gender, identity, sexuality, alienation, desire and loss in a way which at the same time foregrounds the difficulties of communication, objectivity and truth.

For, unlike much of the poetry of the Women's Movement which has gone before, Duffy does not privilege an authenticity of everyday lived experience. While she engages with politics and can easily access some of the devices of realism, at some level Duffy is also uncomfortable with the solutions they provide in her negotiation of the world. And although she clearly understands that it is the responsibility of the poet to attempt to go some way towards understanding and explaining the world in social and political terms, she is also painfully aware of the complexities of such activity. Her interest in a reclamation of the self through memory, and her desire to reconstruct that self through a nostalgic recognition of a state, before language, that can never be articulated or reclaimed, become a temporary escape from the world which she encounters. And yet this sense of psychological exile is never left unbalanced by a political awareness of, for example, the needs of immigrants who face poverty and oppression in Britain today. Likewise, Duffy's use of the dramatic monologue, while posing questions about the nature of self-representation and the fallibility of language, is also a genuine attempt to highlight and give voice to the plight of a disadvantaged other.

Remarkably, Duffy has managed to resist the increasing media hype that surrounds the so-called poetry boom. Her desire, until recently, to remain loyal to the imprint of a small

3

press underpins a poetic which is both tough and tender, which chooses both the lyrical and the narrative, which combines 'high' art with popular culture, the prosaic with the philosophical, the political with the personal, the radical with the poignant, nostalgic, even, sometimes, the knowingly sentimental. Duffy's poetry is intelligent without being exclusive, it is humorous without being glib, direct without being reductive. It is a poetry that is intelligent enough to remember and question the past, while in the most exciting ways it struggles to rethink and rearticulate the new. As Sean O'Brien writes on the jacket of her *Selected Poems*, 'Poetry, like love, depends on a kind of recognition. So often with Duffy does the reader say "Yes, that's it exactly"'. For as well as dramatizing the anxiety of her position as a woman poet at a turning point in the history of women's poetry this century, her work also illustrates the anxieties of the age in which she lives: anxieties about the relationship of the self to the world, about the validity of communication, and the disturbance of gender roles. Duffy's is a remarkable achievement; hers a ground-breaking and original voice.

4

1

Beginnings

...I remember my tongue
shedding its skin like a snake, my voice
in the classroom sounding just like the rest. Do I only think
I lost a river, culture, speech, sense of first space
and the right place? Now, *Where do you come from?*
strangers ask. *Originally?* And I hesitate.

('Originally', *SP* 65–6)

Perhaps not surprisingly, placing Duffy into some neat compart-
ment as a poet is an impossible task. Do we read her as a Scottish
poet? A Scottish woman poet? A feminist poet? A working-class
poet? Is she a political poet, a dramatic poet, or a lyric poet? Of
course, she is all of these things and none of them, testimony to
the fact that the value of the neat pigeonhole is undoubtedly
suspect. What trying to place Duffy in these categories achieves,
however, is that it gives us a way of understanding how she *might*
be positioned, while at the same time highlighting an elusive
quality that haunts her work and often translates into anxieties
about the idea of the unsayable, and the unplaceable.

Duffy's first pamphlet of adolescent poems, *Fleshweathercock*,
was published in 1973 by Howard Sergeant's Outposts Press
when she was just 18. It was not until she was 27 that her second
pamphlet, *Fifth Last Song*, was published by Headland with
accompanying artwork by, among others, Jeff Nuttall, Adrian
Henri and Henry Graham. Subtitled *twenty-one love poems*, it
perhaps owes something to Adrienne Rich's sequence of lesbian
love poems 'Twenty-One Love Poems' which appeared in her *A
Dream of A Common Language: Poems 1974–1977* (1978), and
Neruda's *Twenty Love Poems and a Song of Despair* (English
translation 1969). Although Duffy herself considers it juvenilia,

some of the better poems act as an interesting backdrop to her later work. In the title poem, 'Fifth Last Song' (FLS 8), a desire is expressed for union with the natural world which somehow blurs with the body of a lover.

> I love you rain I kiss you moon
> you hold me sun we sleep stars;
> all seasons are in us and tonight
> we part in bright snow slowly, little cloud,
> grace without shadow, red mouth
> which bites sweeter than apples.
> A clear voice sends new colours
> to the mountains of night, my breast
> is fruit bitten; I love you wind, light.
>
> Forever's a minute and each hour upon us
> over each other. The circle touches itself
> where the hand of my lover is perfect
> as grass. Sun ocean bird stone pause
> to become us, singing one strange note
> from equal distances. I want you planets,
> little flame, you cover me flesh bone hair,
> the sky moans in dark rivers
> for morning and I love you water, air.

There is more than a hint of Coleridge's 'Kubla Khan' here: Duffy's reference to the sun and the snow compare with Coleridge's 'sunny pleasure-dome with caves of ice!'; her circle that 'touches itself / where the hand of my lover is perfect / as grass' recalls Coleridge's Abyssinian maid who sings to 'Weave a circle round him thrice' to warn of the man with 'His flashing eyes, his floating hair!' But we can also hear Dylan Thomas, and an encroaching sense of the surreal as the desire to merge with the natural world is figured through the breast becoming bitten fruit and the lovers who metamorphose into sun, ocean, bird, stone.

In another of these early poems, 'Dream' (FLS 15), we see Duffy drawing visual images from the surrealist painter and collector Roland Penrose:

> DREAM
>
> She has placed bright insects on her eyes
> to beguile him; his city is grey waiting
> for her arrival. When she comes
> butterflies drift out of her, on her thighs

bruises form like dragonflies.
Grass grows on the walls of dull buildings
whilst the wind holds its breath;
from the sky matches fall. She is
picking them up she is striking them,
she is burning all his bridges.
She has placed bright insects on her eyes
and she is flying.

Although not explicitly surrealist in its content, the references in Duffy's poem point to a tradition of surrealist art and writing which has obviously had a strong influence on her early writing. The poem can be interestingly compared to Penrose's painting *Winged Domino: Portrait of Valentine* (1938) which illustrates the cover of the Penguin book of *Surrealist Poetry in English*.[1] The painting shows the bust of a woman. Her skin is blue and her long, waving hair has birds nesting in it. Butterflies or moths settle on her eyes and across her mouth as if they are feeding off her. As its title suggests, 'Dream' works by articulating a set of antithetical objects and placing them in juxtaposition: butterflies are balanced by the more aggressive dragonflies; female assertiveness is balanced by a masculine vulnerability; and in a different way, the relative harmlessness of matches and matchmaking is juxtaposed with violence and fire. Duffy uses the surrealist device of punning on the sound of words: insects as 'in-sex'.

As well as being a poem about a seduction, 'Dream' is charged with the liberation of that seduction. With its references to flight, and its use of punning as a means of liberating alternative meanings, it is difficult to ignore comparison with the work of the writer Hélène Cixous (in particular Cixous's punning on the word *voler*, meaning both 'to fly' and 'to steal'). Cixous's fêting of the hysterical female body as an emancipatory instrument which works against repression can in many ways be seen as similar to surrealist desires to assimilate neglected or repressed feminine qualities. For Cixous, true creativity involves a multiplication of subjectivity. But whereas this otherness is externalized by the surrealists, for Cixous it is internalized and assimilated as desire or loss, the female body thus becoming a potential site of carnivalesque subversions.[2] For Duffy, the female body that is the poem's central image is both subject and object of desire; it controls and is controlled, and its sexuality

7

allows the emergence of a female self. As unrepresentative stylistically as it is of her later work, it is interesting because it marks a vital transition in her work, a transition which sees her abandoning the Romantic in favour of the surreal as a means of expressing and liberating the self in terms of otherness.

*

What, specifically, did surrealism offer Duffy at this early point in her development? As I will discuss in the following chapters, the surreal, like the dramatic monologue, provides a means of projecting a self or selves onto the world in a way that is not immediately or obviously identifiable with the personal. As an aesthetic, surrealism speaks publicly and often extravagantly of experiences which are usually secret, unmentionable or unsayable. Yet even in the extravagance of expression, it manages to retain an element of the mysterious and covert. This sense of surrealism acting like a hinge between self and otherness, the private and the public, the blatant and the covert, the knowable and the unknowable, is of particular relevance to women because of the way it echoes, as well as dramatizes, their own anxieties about speaking or writing in public. Surrealism, through its juxtaposition of the objective and the subjective, the conscious and the unconscious, inner and outer realities, allows the reader to experience the anxiety that fuels its creation. 'Objective reality' is placed in juxtaposition with subjective truths, and during this process the self becomes objectified, becoming both self and other. It is surrealism's transformation of the very category of the personal – its attempt to universalize experience by appealing to the unconscious as a medium that translates experience – which is of key importance to women who perhaps wish to express a personal female experience but also want to keep it secret or encode it.

Although the influence of surrealism is not so directly apparent in her later work, it serves as a crucial underpinning to Duffy's development as a writer. Duffy's aesthetic derives directly from surrealist practices, which also filtered through into the work of her contemporaries and friends, the Underground poets of the 1960s and 1970s with whom she associated while at university in Liverpool. This can be seen particularly in the work of Adrian Henri, whose poems at the time were influenced by the Beat poets Ginsberg, Corso and Ferlinghetti. Henri has described the phenomenon of Underground poetry as being something which represented

a certain bridging of the gap between 'high-brow' and 'pop' cultures by concert performance of poetry with pop-music (something other members of the Underground attempted by giving performances of poetry and jazz). Though an infinitely more modest effort than those early French pioneers ... this may still be seen in the context of the Surrealist aim to transform society through poetry.[3]

In 1983 Duffy won first prize in the National Poetry Competition. A brief but revealing article in *Poetry Review* (1984),[4] appearing under the title 'Woman Wins', and a rather fuzzy picture of Duffy standing before a microphone, not only contextualizes the critical reception of Duffy's work at the point at which it is becoming recognizably hers, but also neatly illustrates an underlying distrust of surrealism, and failure to negotiate a new and emerging talent. It is evidence also of the fact that the idea of a woman both being a poet and winning a competition was still a new phenomenon, although the Northern Irish poet Medbh McGuckian had also won the competition in 1979. The review begins:

The National Poetry Society Competition has again (see last year) failed to unearth convincing winners from a total of 12,000 submissions. The first prize of £2,000 was awarded by Gillian Clarke, Vernon Scannell and Kevin Crossley-Holland to 'Whoever She Was' by Carol Ann Duffy. This is quite an effective evocation of some eerie moments in the relation between motherhood and childhood, but much of the detail is predictable, and the language is not very interesting, so that the poem doesn't improve with repeated readings. It is notable for having more full stops than lines:

> Mummy, say the little voices of the ghosts
> Of children on the telephone. Mummy.
> > . . . when they
> think of me, I'm bending over them at night
> to kiss. Perfume. Rustle of silk. Sleep tight.

Apart from the obvious misogyny of the review (women and '[un]convincing winners' become synonymous), what is most interesting is the way it chooses to exclude the surreal elements of the poem completely.[5] The four lines immediately preceding

9

the lines the reviewer has chosen to quote read:

> They see me always as a flickering figure
> on a shilling screen. Not real. My hands,
> still wet, spout wooden pegs. I smell the apples
> burning as I hang the washing out.

The next lines to be omitted are:

> A row of paper dollies, cleaning wounds
> or boiling eggs for soldiers. The chant
> of magic words repeatedly. I do not know.
> Perhaps tomorrow. If we're very good.
> The film is on a loop. Six silly ladies
> torn in half by baby fists.

(SP 13)

The reviewer seems to object to the poem because it fails to speak in a high poetic language for which the joint second-prize-winning entries are especially notable: one by a 'Mr. Chadwick' who is 'an advisor with the Poetry Society's Critical Service' and writes a sestina with 'Plenty of ear-catching verbs' . . . (shriek, bleat, screel), good colour-sense, and sufficient ingenuity'. This particular reception of Duffy's poem – which is placed outside the tradition on account of its surrealism, its adoption of another voice, its subsequent refusal to use the high language traditionally associated with poetry, and, not least on account of its author's sex and subject matter, seems an important indicator of prevailing attitudes towards women's writing, surrealism and a new, more demotic, poetry which does not use traditional forms.

Duffy's interest in surrealism is made most explicit in a later poem, 'Translation' (SM 39) in which Duffy makes direct allusion to the surrealist Antonin Artaud:

> TRANSLATION
>
> 'All writing is garbage' Artaud
> She wore gloves, red to the elbow, sipped
> at a dry martini, dry-eyed, said *I have come*
> *to confess. Do you want my love?* The old cathedral
> exploded into bells, scattering gulls at the sky
> like confetti. But no wedding. Then? The hunchback
> swung on the one-armed bandit, slack eyes following
> bright uneatable fruit, cranking *Bugger bugger bugger*

10

from stale breath. Later she held a dun root
on a scarlet palm, real satin, her lover's eyes
dark as a bell-tower, mouth bruising O O on the night.
When he pushed into her it was the gambler, crippled,
she invented. Lick me from the navel outwards
darkly in damp circles tell me strange half-truths
from your strange mind babe babe baby.

Duffy's title may also refer to the work of the philosopher Willard Quine, whose work on ideas of translation addresses key philosophical issues concerning the relationship between word and object, and the 'meaning' of words. Although there is a narrative that runs from beginning to end in the poem – the confession of love and the seduction – we see in this progression the disintegration of speech: from the confession of love at the beginning of the poem, to the explosion of bells, the repetition of the word bugger which echoes the noise of the one-arm bandit, to the mouth which bruises OO, to the end of the poem where speech has become a mute communication of the tongue which silently licks its 'strange half-truths'. In the world of the poem, objects are both themselves and other: dry refers to a taste as well as a look in the eye, the one-armed bandit is both the fruit machine and the crippled gambler who plays it, the fruit on the fruit machine is bright but inedible, a representation but not the thing itself. Focusing on the fruit machine, the game of chance in which pictures are randomly organized, Duffy seems to be playing with the idea of the chance of meaning itself. The final image of the lover licking the navel of the confessor constructs at the end of the poem an image of circularity – the navel, the mouth, the damp circles the lover makes with his tongue – leaving us with a literally hermeneutic circle.

The quotation from Artaud which Duffy uses as an epigraph comes from his tract 'Nerve Scales', a prose piece about the accessing of a creative self through automatism. Near the beginning of the essay, Artaud describes his attempts to reach a mental state that will allow him to create. He writes:

> I have always been struck by the mind's obstinacy in wanting to think in terms of measurements of areas, in fastening on arbitrary states of things so as to think. Thinking is segments, crystalloids, so that each form of existence remains fixed in the beginning and thought does not communicate with objects instantaneously and

11

uninterrupted. But this fixation, this immobilisation, this sort of monumentalisation of the soul occurs BEFORE THOUGHT, so to speak. Obviously these are the right conditions for creativity.... Surreality is like a sort of osmotic contraction, a sort of inverted communication. Far from any weakening in control, on the contrary control seems to me more assured, but control which instead of acting remains on guard and reverts contact with day to day reality and allows more subtle and rarefied contacts, contacts reduced to a thread which catches fire but never breaks.[6]

In her use of juxtaposition Duffy is also attempting to highlight how meaning can be created by context, that within the structures of a poem meaning can be generated through contrast, colour, sound, and position. Words do not mean simply in themselves, she seems to suggest, but are subject to a continuous act of translation.

Duffy's major preoccupations during the early 1980s, and as late as *Selling Manhattan* (1987) in which 'Translation' was published, arise from her interest in avant-garde and surrealist art, and the philosophers of language whom she studied as an undergraduate. Her interest in surrealism is in many ways symptomatic of her wish to revitalize language in a way which does not depend on a notion of the authority of a speaker or the authenticity of experience. Central to this project is a desire to think about ways in which the everyday language can be revitalized within a poem. In an interview of 1988, we find Duffy explaining how she uses cliché by placing it in italics in juxtaposition to other parts of the poem:

> If I was to write a love poem which said 'When I look at you I'm over the moon, let's go to bed and make a spoon' which are things I do say in real speech, as a poem it would look banal or awful. But if you can bring things into a poem at a particular stage, almost ordering it musically, you can perhaps bring out what you hear in them anyway. So I would often put a cliché in italics, or a fragment of speech that seems very ordinary, next to something else in the hope that it would nudge the reader into seeing it the way I do....
>
> I'm not interested in words like 'plash', you know, Seamus Heaney words, interesting words. I don't like them. I like to use simple words but in a complicated way so that you can see the lies and truths within the poem. And it is for myself as well; it's a way of revealing to myself what is truthful and what isn't.... You can put little spotlights on phrases, like clichés, that will show how although they

look like a plastic rose in fact they've got roots underneath. They have meaning. And I'm interested in that because I don't talk, when I'm talking about life and death matters – things that are important to me, in anything other than very plain simple language. And no-one else does. And I think poetry needs that.... When you read a poem to an audience it's possible to show these things, but in print the only way is italics or capitals or bold typeface.[7]

It's interesting to compare this with Henri's 'Notes on Painting and Poetry', which acts as an afterword to his collection *Tonight at Noon*, and in which Henri discusses his practice as both a poet and an artist. In one passage he aligns the new forms of poetry with surrealist practice in their aim to rid language or art of worn-out modes of language or presentations of the image which easily become havens for cliché:

The cliché is a living piece of language that has gone dead through overwork. At any time it can be energized or revitalized. Often by changing its context, putting it in an alien context, contradicting its apparent meaning. This applies equally to the visual arts: much of Dada/Surrealism and Pop Art consists of doing just this. Breton spoke of 'certain forms of association hitherto neglected': Lautréamont's 'beautiful as the unexpected meeting, on a dissecting table, of a sewing-machine and an umbrella' is often rightly quoted as a definition of Surrealist procedures. Meret Oppenheim's 'Fur-covered Cup, Saucer and Spoon' or Man Ray's 'Cadeau' are perhaps the best-known examples of this process.[8]

Duffy's highlighting or 'spotlighting' of words warns the reader not to take them for granted as part of some univocal construction of an authoritative or dominant world view. In Duffy's poems clichés can become more than themselves. For, in making that representation of failure part of the 'truth' of language, what it can and cannot say, Duffy makes a case for using language in a poem in a way that incorporates a range of registers and voices, allowing the poem to take on subtle shades of irony and self-knowing. She takes her interest in the cliché to a surreal extreme in 'The Cliché Kid' (*MT* 18). Here the desire to speak in clichés represents an anxiety about both speaking and writing, as she reassembles clichés and lines of her previous poems, and presents them as a symptom of her distress to an imaginary doctor:

Give me a break. Don't let me pine for that first love,
that faint down on the cheeks, that easy laugh
in my ears, in my lonesome heart, the day I had to leave...

Sweet Jesus, Doc, I worry I'll miss when a long time dead
the smell the smell the smell of the baby's head,
the fresh-baked grass, dammit, the new-mown bread.

The cliché offers a double way of telling; it is both failure and truth. It's important at this point, then, to note how Duffy's interest in surrealism, and one of its primary devices, juxtaposition, leads directly towards her experimentation with polyphony and her distrust of language as mediator between idea and object. For Duffy an exploration of the relationship between language and experience always dramatizes a gap between signifier and signified; between what is about to be said, and what is then said; between the possibility of what might be said, and what can never be said. And this distrust of language leads her to an aesthetic that privileges experience over the telling of the experience:

Away and see the things that words give a name to, the flight
of syllables, wingspan stretching a noun. Test words
wherever they live; listen and touch, smell, believe.

(*SP* 107)

'Nothing's the same as anything else', she states in the same poem. Yet it is the duty of the artist to try and bridge this gap, to mediate experience through the telling. It is to these ideas of truth and representation that I will now turn.

*

Duffy's first full-length collection, *Standing Female Nude*, published by Anvil in 1985, marks the definitive move in her writing from the personal and Romantic lyric to a dramatic one. The title poem, 'Standing Female Nude' (*SP* 20–1), is a monologue in the voice of an artist's model, and focuses the preoccupations of the volume as a whole: power, the relationships between men and women, and the difficulty of mediating experience and representing the world in language and through art. The poem begins:

Six hours like this for a few francs.
Belly nipple arse in the window light,
he drains the colour from me. Further to the right,
Madame. And do try to be still.

14

I shall be represented analytically and hung
in great museums. The bourgeoisie will coo
at such an image of a river-whore. They call it Art.

Maybe. He is concerned with volume, space.
I with the next meal....

The use of colloquialisms at the beginning of the poem, 'Belly
nipple arse', serves simultaneously to destabilize the idea of
who is speaking: is this the voice of the artist or the model? The
representation of the body in language, with its free-flowing
non-punctuated sentence, is deliberately ambiguous: does this,
for example, allow body parts a sense of movement or liquidity,
or does it have the effect of separating and commodifying them
so that the painter's or model's perspective of the model
becomes, in effect, pornographic? Do the terms used to describe
the body empower and desexualize, or cheapen and objectify?
We find a later poem, 'Mouth with Soap' (*SM* 44) railing against
'The Censor, clacking a wooden tongue. Watch out / for the tight
vocabulary of living death', so perhaps speaking of the body in
these terms seems to suggest a kind of liberation from the
strictures of bourgeois values. The strength of the poem is that it
is impossible to say. For while power relationships between men
and women are being interrogated, so also is the nature and
value of their representation.

Duffy's use of the forename 'Georges' in the poem indicates
that she may be alluding to an early painting by the Cubist
Braque. In some ways, in his renegotiation of space, Braque
seems to offer Duffy a positive model of representation which
can be compared to her project in the revitalization of the
dramatic monologue. As John Golding writes, Braque's painting
is interested in the 'rejection of traditional, single viewpoint
perspective':

> The rejection of traditional, single viewpoint perspective was as
> essential to Braque's materialization of the spatial sensations as it
> was to Picasso's desire to convey a multiplicity of information in
> every painted object....it was Braque's purpose to bring...space
> forward towards the spectator, to invite him in to explore it, to touch
> it optically.[9]

Throughout the poem, the model sees herself as other; but she also sees the painter seeing her. The placing of the word 'hung' at the end of the line is playing with the idea of art as a living death for the model. Yet when the model herself sees an image of woman, and this, in splendid contrast, is an image of the future Queen of England gazing at *her* shape, it is as a prophecy in the tea leaves, notably non-representational and fragmentary, and not unlike the painter's way of seeing:

> ...He is concerned with volume, space.
> I with the next meal. You're getting thin,
> Madame, this is not good. My breasts hang
> slightly low, the studio is cold. In the tea-leaves
> I can see the Queen of England gazing
> on my shape. Magnificent, she murmurs,
> moving on....

The final line of the poem, spoken by the model as she is leaving, 'It does not look like me', can be read as both redemptive and pitiful and anticipates many of Duffy's later poems in which her personae look at themselves in mirrors but fail to recognize themselves. Is it that the woman has not been caught by the male gaze, or is it simply that the male gaze has misrepresented her, left her unrecognizable to herself?

This theme of self-recognition and the failure of representation, as pointed to in the final lines of 'Standing Female Nude', is one which runs unresolved throughout the volume, whether it is representation through painting, film, photography or language. On the opposite page to 'Standing Female Nude', 'Poem in Oils' (*SFN* 47) equates the 'soundless shadows' which 'fall from trees' with brushstrokes. The shadows are both themselves and an image of leaves, as well as the means by which they are represented, the shape of the brush and the leaves superimposed on each other. 'Is this what I see?' asks the voice of the poem, only to answer 'No, but this is the process of seeing'. It is this emphasis on process, an emphasis which realism rejects in favour of a final and unified vision, which, increasingly, Duffy seeks to explore.

2

Masquerades

> ...Years stand outside on the street
> looking up to an open window, black as our mouth
> which utters its tuneless song. The ghosts of ourselves,
> behind and before us, throng in a mirror, blind,
> laughing and weeping. They know who we are.
>
> ('Close', *SP* 118)

Knowing who we are, and finding a way to tell ourselves, are two of Duffy's central concerns. In questioning the ways in which we are represented, she also addresses the difficulties of knowing the self through otherness. As I suggested in the previous chapter, this is a questioning for which the dramatic monologue is particularly useful. In her use of the form, Duffy inherits a tradition from Browning, Laforgue, Eliot and W. S. Graham. Importantly she can also be grouped alongside three other contemporary women poets: U. A. Fanthorpe (b. 1929), who reconstituted the dramatic monologue for feminist ends in the late 1970s and early 1980s; and two Scottish poets, Liz Lochhead (b. 1947), and Jackie Kay (b. 1961), whose *The Adoption Papers* (Bloodaxe, 1991) directly acknowledges Duffy's 'help and encouragement'.

Primarily the dramatic monologue presents a way of bringing the poet's self into the public world, while simultaneously denying responsibility, and masking presence – it is not, after all, the poet who is speaking but the character who is being portrayed. Yet while being a mode of writing that appears to destabilize the relationship between the poet and the poem's speaking voice, the 'I' of the monologue exhibits an over-determined and objectified selfhood symptomatic of anxieties about claiming any kind of subject position. In many ways the monologue is a method of disclaiming or dislocating oneself

17

from a subject position. Robert Langbaum concedes that the 'standard account of the dramatic monologue is that Browning and Tennyson conceived it as a reaction against the romantic confessional style', and cites the disclaimer to Browning's 1842 *Dramatic Lyrics*: 'so many utterances of so many imaginary persons, not mine'.[1]

One important reason why the monologue may appeal to women as a form may come from an already pervasive sense of the everyday artificiality of the construction of women's role. Isobel Armstrong has shown that it was in fact women poets who were the first to use the monologue as a way of negotiating the 'problem' of femininity. Writing on these nineteenth-century women poets, Armstrong comments on the phenomenon of the adopted female voice in the monologue, which illustrates the woman poet who is:

> in control of her objectification and at the same time anticipates the strategy of objectifying women by being beforehand with it and circumventing masculine representations.[2]

This sense of the artificiality of the construction of the persona in the monologue is examined by Duffy in 'The Dummy' (*SP* 36); but rather than examine the persona of the ventriloquist directly, Duffy gives the dummy a life and voice of its own:

> Balancing me with your hand up my back, listening
> to the voice you gave me croaking for truth, you keep
> me at it. Your lips don't move, but your eyes look
> desperate as hell. Ask me something difficult.
>
> Maybe we could sing together? Just teach me
> the right words, I learn fast. Don't stare like that.
> I'll start where you leave off. I can't tell you
> anything if you don't throw me a cue line. We're dying

As a comment on the operation of the dramatic monologue, Duffy deconstructs her own poetic device in the final line of the poem: '*Come on*. You can do getter than that, can't you?' The irony of the poem depends on the reader knowing that Duffy is satirizing her own adoption of other 'imaginary voices' for which, by 1987, she was already well known. In doing this she creates and highlights a reflexive loop running between the poet and the ventriloquist. The ventriloquist's dummy becomes a mirror which enacts and reflects selfhood. Jane E. Thomas writes:

On one level this poem can be seen as a study in mental breakdown in which conflicting aspects of a personality wage war on one another. Films such as *The Great Gabbo* (1929), *Dead of Night* (1945) and *Devil Doll* (1964) have all used the device of the Ventriloquist whose dummy comes to life to dramatise the trauma of schizophrenia. At the same time anyone familiar with Freudian theories of the unconscious might see Duffy's dummy as a metaphor for that dark repository of repressions and socially taboo desires which constantly irrupts into our conscious existence in the forms of dreams, fantasies and 'Freudian slips'. If we were to analyze the poem in the light of Lacan's re-interpretation of Freud it would appear to dramatize the split between the speaking subject (the Ventriloquist) and the subject position which allows it to articulate its experience of reality (the dummy) and which in doing so constructs that experience independently of the individual.[3]

In a later poem, 'Small Female Skull' (*SP* 109–10), Duffy uses a more overtly surreal conceit to illustrate her preoccupation with interrogating an objectified or alienated self. Like 'The Dummy', a split in consciousness between the speaking and the bodily self is dramatized, but here the skull becomes a trope for both the self and 'a friend of mine', the lost lover who is other. The poem explores a heightened sense of the fragile and incomprehensible nature of existence:

> With some surprise, I balance my small female skull in my hands.
> What is it like? An ocarina? Blow in its eye.
> It cannot cry, holds my breath only as long as I exhale,
> mildly alarmed now, into the hole where the nose was,
> press my ear to its grin. A vanishing sigh.
>
> For some time, I sit on the lavatory seat with my head
> in my hands, appalled. It feels much lighter than I'd thought;
> the weight of a deck of cards, a slim volume of verse,
> But with something else, as though it could levitate.
> Disturbing.
> So why do I kiss it on the brow, my warm lips to its papery
> bone,
>
> and take it to the mirror to ask for a gottle of geer?

The literal and the metaphorical, the real and the surreal, intermingle as the poem puns on the idea of holding one's head in one's hands. With its parodic echoes of the gravediggers' scene in *Hamlet*, this act represents an existential questioning ('to be or not to be'); but it is also a mourning of the loss of the lover with whom the self has so strongly identified. The use of the word 'papery' in the question 'so why do I kiss it on the brow, my warm lips to its papery bone' perhaps suggests a metaphor for the transition of this poem from mouth to page itself; and there is surely here, too, an echo of Webster through Eliot, of the 'skull beneath the skin'.[4] Kissing skulls in Jacobean tragedies is a dangerous occupation, and dangerous here also is the interrogation of the self in the poem. The poem dramatizes a confrontation with the self as other, as well as the loss of a beloved who is so loved that she constitutes a loss of the self:

Downstairs they will think I have lost my mind. No. I only weep
into these two holes here, or I'm grinning back at the joke, this is
a friend of mine. See, I hold her face in trembling, passionate hands

However, as we have seen, Duffy does not always adopt a female voice in her monologues. Her interest in the other as a projection of the self is equalled by an interest in the psychology of characters whose gender and attitude is at a far remove from her own. In 'You Jane' (*SFN* 34) we are presented with a blatant act of ventriloquism as Duffy takes on the voice of the ultimate in male macho:

At night I fart a Guinness smell against the wife
who snuggles up to me after I've given her one
after the Dog and Fox. It's all muscle. You can punch
my gut and wait forever till I flinch. Try it.
Man of the house. Master in my own home. Solid.

Look at that bicep. Dinner on the table
and a clean shirt, but I respect her point of view.
She's borne me two in eight years, knows
when to button it. Although she's run a bit to fat
she still bends over of a weekend in suspenders.

At one level the monologue is providing the poet with a way of incorporating otherness into the poetic utterance without appearing either phoney, voyeuristic or directly judgemental. Language is being used in a way that is traditionally inappropriate both to femininity and to poetry's high language. But there is a sense that the persona is not fully adopted. In spite of what seems to be an adoption of a discourse self-consciously other than the poet's, in the last two lines there is a moment of unexpected return to the poetic, which indicates a kind of slippage, so that what we really seem to be reading is a third-person account:

> I wake half-conscious with a hard-on, shove it in.
> She don't complain. When I feel, I feel here
> where the purple vein in my neck throbs.

Is Duffy, in the elision between her 'own' voice and that of 'other', asking us to rethink our opinion of the 'he-man'? The purple vein is, after all, as much an image of potency and aggression in its throbbing as it is of vulnerability.

Duffy's interest in 'the impossible case', the bored potential killer of 'Education for Leisure' (*SP* 11), the snow thief of 'Stealing' (*SP* 49–50) or the psychiatric patient in 'And How Are We Today' (*SP* 42), reaches its culmination in 'Psychopath' (*SP* 43–6), and we see again a connection being established between the voice of the poet and the monologist whose voice she 'takes on'.

'Psychopath' constructs a persona through memory and fragments of remembered language – fragments of cliché, nursery rhyme and popular song are pitted against flashbacks of the killer's early childhood and sexual experiences. The psychopath, although the most extreme of Duffy's personae, exhibits a similar lack of sensitivity, and an extreme gullibility to patriarchal constructs of masculinity. The trauma of his childhood, his father who leaves because he finds his wife with the Rent man, and his sexual experience in the woods at the age of 12, becomes elided with the images of the local girl he later seduces:

> Dirty Alice flicked my dick out when I was twelve.
> She jeered. I nicked a quid and took her to the spinney.
> I remember the wasps, the sun blazing as I pulled
> her knickers down. I touched her and I went hard,
> but she grabbed my hand and used that, moaning...
> She told me her name on the towpath, holding the fish
> in a small sack of water. We walked away from the lights...
> She'd come too far with me now. She looked back, once.

The poem perhaps owes something of its inspiration to Henri's 'Fairground Poem' which appeared in his collection *Tonight at Noon* (1968).[5] Towards the end of Henri's poem, in which we are privy to the thoughts of a predatory male, we hear the lines 'Deafened by music from all sides/ *Johnny, remember'...*/ *She's a square,/ Baby, I don't care...*' The '*Johnny, remember*' line is picked up in Duffy's 'Psychopath':

> Let me make myself crystal. With a good-looking girl crackling in four petticoats, you feel like a king. She rode past me on a wooden horse, laughing, and the air sang *Johnny Remember Me.* I turned the world faster, flash.

The psychopath sees himself in terms of the heroes of Hollywood films – James Dean, Marlon Brando, Elvis, Humphrey Bogart. His projection of self is itself a masquerade of masculinity. At three points in the poem the psychopath sees himself as a reflection (a motif which perhaps reminds us here of a technique used notably by Fritz Lang in films such as *M*, 1931, starring Peter Lorre, which tells the story of a compulsive child murderer: in the first two lines, 'I run my metal comb through the D.A. and pose/ my reflection between dummies in the window of Burton's'; and then in stanza two, 'My breath wipes me from the looking-glass'; and eventually, in the final stanza, the persona faces himself in the mirror and fails to identify with his own reflection, 'My reflection sucks a sour Woodbine and buys me a drink. Here's/ looking at you'. But who is looking at who? As Ian Gregson argues, the poem

> suggests the poet's voice as much as it might the psychopath's – 'my shoes scud sparks against the night' is imagist in rhythm and in the way it juxtaposes light and dark, and sounds like something that would be more comfortable in the third person rather than the first. 'Psychopath' works...not through the simple verisimilitude of its mimicry but more through something closer to parody....The shifts that are involved as the reader watches the psychopath watching himself are important because they draw attention to the question of how what is being seen is being interpreted.[6]

The persona is constructed as self-conscious and his articulation of that self-consciousness becomes part of the irony drawn up in the process of writing the monologue itself. Calling the poem 'Psychopath', Duffy presents us with a character about whom we are not asked to declare some kind of moral judgement; stating at the beginning that this is a monologue of a figure who is (or must be?) mad, the judgement has already been made. Yet this is a judgement which is both accusation and exoneration. It's interesting to compare this with an interview Duffy gave in 1991 in which she talks about her use of the monologue. She explains:

> You asked about giving voice for others. Clearly on one level, that is the case – but there is an initial, and often quite powerful, empathy or identification, which has to occur, does occur, before one would bother at all. I come from a working-class background which, in many areas, was inarticulate. Not politically, but on those levels where one speaks of the personal, the feelings, the private inner life. What I mean is that language was often perceived as embarrassing or dangerous. The dramatic monologues I've written ... are, yes, objective; but closer to me as the writer than would appear.[7]

Throughout her work, Duffy demonstrates a fascination with representation, and a key image for her is one of the self who looks in the mirror. In 'Whoever She Was' (*SP* 13–14) a woman has been effaced by the swamping demands of her role as mother:

> Whoever she was, forever their wide eyes watch her
> as she shapes a church and steeple in the air.
> She cannot be myself and yet I have a box
> of dusty presents to confirm that she was here.
> You remember the little things. Telling stories
> or pretending to be strong. Mummy's never wrong.
> *You open your dead eyes to look in the mirror*
> *which they are holding to your mouth.*

And in a monologue, 'Recognition' (*SP* 40–1), in which a middle-aged woman fails to recognize her reflection in a window:

> . . . I had to rush out,
> blind in a hot flush, and bumped
>
> into an anxious, dowdy matron
> who touched the cold mirror
> and stared at me. Stared
> and said I'm sorry sorry sorry.

As Thomas suggested in the piece I quoted earlier, this preoccupation with the self who looks and the reflected self who is other recalls Lacan's by now well-known theory of the *stade du miroir*. According to Lacan, the child's entry into language depends on this moment of recognition of itself as

23

both self and other. The Imaginary state, which precedes it, is a stage in which the infant is speechless, with little motor coordination; it is unable to identify its image with itself. This state, as Jan Montefiore ably demonstrates, is of vital importance in our reading of poetry by women, not simply our reading of Duffy.[8] Drawing on the work of Luce Irigaray, Montefiore argues that

> If women are to find their own identity and meaning, it is necessary first to repossess our primitive love for the mother: the baby's first, pre-Oedipal bond. In other words, we need to repossess our identities through reclaiming as women our lost Imaginary state. But at present we are still in exile.[9]

As we shall see in the remainder of this book, it is this sense of exile, coupled with a prevailing sense of the inadequacy of language to represent experience, which runs throughout Duffy's work. And although Montefiore's reading of Lacan, and Irigaray's essays in *Speculum* and *Ce Sexe qui n'en est pas un*, concentrate on the love poem (and we shall come to that in the next chapter), I would argue that this model is equally important in our reading of Duffy's monologues.

For Lacan, both men and women partake in an exaggerated construction of sexual difference which is brought into being at the entry into the Symbolic, when the child sees itself not only as 'I' but as 'he' or 'she'. Lacan's concept of difference is drawn in part from the concept of 'masquerade' suggested by the analyst Joan Riviere in her seminal essay 'Womanliness as a masquerade' (1929). In this important, although not unresolved essay, Riviere sees womanhood as a role *adopted* by the woman as a way of concealing 'her masculinity from the masculine audience she wants to castrate':[10]

> Womanliness therefore could be assumed and worn as a mask, both to hide the possession of masculinity and to avert the reprisals expected if she was found to possess it – much as a thief will turn out his pockets and ask to be searched to prove that he has not stolen the goods.[11]

For Riviere, masquerade, the turning out of the pockets by the thief, and its covert reference to genitals, carries with it an underlying anxiety about female lack. Returning to Irigaray, it is interesting to see her addressing this idea of the mask in 'The

Blind Spot in an Old Dream Symmetry', in which she takes Freud to task for a series of assumptions about femininity in his 1933 lecture 'Femininity'. Freud writes:

> Shame, which is considered to be a feminine characteristic par excellence but is far more a matter of convention than might be supposed, has as its purpose, we believe, concealment of genital deficiency. We are not forgetting that at a later time shame takes on other functions. It seems that women have made few contributions to the discoveries and inventions in the history of civilisation; there is, however, one technique which they may have invented – that of plaiting and weaving.... Nature would seem to have given the model which this achievement imitates by causing the growth at maturity of the pubic hair that conceals the genitals. The step that remained to be taken lay in making the threads adhere to one another, while on the body they stick to the skin and are only matted together. If you reject this idea as fantastic and regard my belief in the influence of a lack of a penis on the configuration of femininity as an *ideé fixe*, I am of course defenceless.[12]

Irigaray's response to Freud and Lacan, while not rejecting their theoretical positions outright, attempts to rethink the implication of the woven veil which masks the little boy's horror of maternal lack. For Irigaray, this 'wrapping up', this 'restoring to wholeness', means woman is alienated from her body. Drawing on Marx's *Capital*, she argues that this disguise 'preserves the "value" from a just evaluation. And allows the "exchange" of goods "without knowledge" of their effective value'.[13] Thus the body becomes a commodity, and the woman's concept of otherness is therefore twofold, negotiated not through the self, but mediated through an appropriated other. Fascinatingly, in an interview in 1988, Duffy appears to echo Freud, and the debate he provokes, when discussing her use of the monologue:

> It also comes back to – and this is a sort of vanity – the things women poets can and can't do. For quite a long time even into this decade we've been allowed certain areas of subject matter, like children, what bastards men are, looms: all these things that appear in late seventies, early eighties women's anthologies. But I haven't got any children and I don't define myself entirely as a woman; I'm not interested in weaving.[14]

In an important, but I think coincidental way, Duffy's reference to looms and weaving, and her rejection of a stereotype of womanhood, highlights an anxiety about the way in which to represent the poetic self. Duffy does not want to be seen to write like a 'woman poet' (and I think it is important to emphasize that it is the term 'woman poet', and not woman which I use here). Might it be that in her use of the dramatic monologue Duffy is necessarily very much interested in weaving as an act of self-preservation, in attempting to cover the 'shame' of her position as a woman poet – that she is in fact deeply implicated in the act of masking her femininity, hiding what is perceived as her 'lack' within the literary tradition? As Irigaray continues: 'woman weaves to sustain the disavowal of her sex'.[15]

Such readings of masquerade throw considerable light on women's use of the monologue, which allows them to repeatedly present themselves as both self and other, subject and object; to speak in ways and about subject matter deemed, because of gender and/or class, inappropriate not only for art, but for representation within a public forum. In this way, Duffy's use of the monologue works as a successful strategy to countermand as well as articulate some of the difficulties which arise when she seeks to adopt a subject position as both a woman and a poet.

Duffy's most recent collection of poems *The World's Wife*, revises fairy tale, history and myth, and reworks it into contemporary feminist fables in ways reminiscent of Anne Sexton's reworking of fairy tales, *Transformations* (1971), Angela Carter's *The Bloody Chamber* (1979), and U. A. Fanthorpe's case-history poems in *Side Effects* (1978) and her Shakespeare's women sequence in *Standing To* (1982). Duffy's return to the politicized writing of the Women's Movement in the 1970s is in some ways an extraordinary one, perhaps in part enabled by a new confidence arising from the positive reception of her work. However, the revisioning of a mythic past also provides Duffy with a way of mediating the personal at the same time as channelling her political ideas. It is interesting, for example, to see Sexton referring to her version of Grimm as

a departure from my usual style ... they lack the intensity and perhaps some of the confessional force of my previous work.... Some of the poems are grim. It would ... be a lie to say that they weren't about me, because they are just as much about me as my other poetry.[16]

As a whole, *The World's Wife* presents us with what might best be described as a metaphorical autobiography. Duffy has spoken about her intention to 'use history and myth and popular culture and elements from the cinema and literature, but also to anchor it in a deeply personal soil and make an entertainment'.[17] The collection begins with the image of the would-be poet as 'Little Red Cap', the girl seductress of the older male poet, the wolf, 'A paperback in his hairy paw,/red wine staining his bearded jaw' (*WW*, 3). This variation on Grimm overlays the retelling of the story with what appears to be a combination of veiled autobiography and a desire to make of that something more universally symbolic in relation to male and female access to the word and the creative process. The story of 'Little Red Cap' has been commented on by a variety of psychoanalytic thinkers. Eric Fromm sees the story as written by Grimm as a 'story of triumph by man-hating women, ending with their victory, exactly the opposite of the Oedipus myth, which lets the male emerge victorious from this battle.'[18] The relationship between wolf and Little Red Cap is what allows Little Red Cap to write, for 'breath of the wolf in my ear, was the love poem' (*WW* 3) and 'Words, words were truly alive, in the head/warm, beating, frantic, winged, music and blood' (*WW* 4). The mating between the sixteen year old 'babe' and the wolf (for whom we can perhaps read the male literary tradition) allows creativity, but also palls as the woman poet becomes disillusioned. The murder of the wolf which, with one chop 'scrotum to throat' reveals 'the glistening, virgin white of my grandmother's bones', allows her to free symbolically an older female version of herself. The apprentice poet gives up her virginity so that she can enter the 'cave of words.'[19]

In 'Mrs Aesop' (*SP* 141–2) Duffy draws on the notorious case of the American woman, Loretta Bobbett, who cut off her husband's penis. The dictats of Mr Aesop's moral universe become the cliché of contemporary life, and to prevent the tale being told Aesop's long-suffering wife threatens to castrate her tedious husband. Male narratives (equated with the phallus) are literally threatened with being cut off in their prime:

> ...I gave him a fable one night
> about a little cock that wouldn't crow, a razor-sharp axe
> with a heart blacker than the pot that called the kettle.
> *I'll cut off your tail all right*, I said, *to save my face.*

Fables here represent both themselves (the little cockerel) and the masculine (the metaphorical penis/cock), so that, in the act of telling the fable, the tale comes to represent the tail or penis. It is only by stopping the story, and removing, or threatening to remove, the penis, that any sense of female identity is preserved. More interesting still is that the pun on this 'saving of face' (which establishes identity, but simultaneously also prevents female shame) is equated with castrating (or making female) the male.

In 'Mrs Tiresias' (*SP* 137–40) Duffy continues humorously to lampoon stereotypical male behaviour while also throwing into question politicized concerns about women's bodies and their rights. Mrs Tiresias, who finds her husband has suddenly turned into a woman, must cope with his inabilities 'to learn' femininity:

> Life has to go on.
>
> I put it about that he was a twin
> and this was his sister
>
> come down to live
> while he himself
> was working abroad.
>
> And at first I tried to be kind;
> blow-drying his hair till he learnt to do it himself,
> lending him clothes till he started to shop for his own,
> sisterly, holding his soft new shape in my arms all night.
>
> Then he started his period.
>
> One week in bed.
> Two doctors in.
> Three painkillers four times a day.
>
> And later
> a letter
> to the powers-that-be
> demanding full-paid menstrual leave twelve weeks per year.
> I see him now,
> his selfish pale face peering at the moon
> through the bathroom window.
> *The curse*, he said, *the curse*.
>
> *Don't kiss me in public,*

28

he snapped the next day,
I don't want people getting the wrong idea.

It got worse.

The poem itself enacts (more explicitly than usual for Duffy) a version of masquerade – the man who becomes the woman, but who is inauthentic, and who although presenting a version of the feminine, cannot speak as a woman. As the poem progresses Mrs Tiresias watches as her 'husband' corrupts his new-found identity:

> . . . on TV
> telling the women out there
> how, as a woman himself,
> he knew how we felt.

> His flirt's smile.

> The one thing he never got right
> was the voice.
> A cling-peach slithering out from its tin.

It is Tiresias's lips which give away his masculinity and, at the end of the poem, fruit – as an image of both the mouth and the female genitals – becomes a metaphor for both sex between women, and speech:

> [I]. . . saw him picture
> her bite,
> her bite at the fruit of my lips,
> and hear
> my red wet cry in the night

This move towards the dramatic monologue in Duffy's newest poems seems to suggest a double strategy. On the one hand, the monologues are probably the most overtly feminist of her *œuvre*; on the other, they are also fantastically removed from reality. As such, they allow Duffy to encode the personal within the characters from myth and history, as well as making feminist statements about the absence of women from history, or their misrepresentation.

3

Love Poems:
A Place Called Home

I love, you love, so does he –
long live English Poetry.
Four o'clock is time for tea,
I'll be Mother, who'll be me?
('Alphabet for Auden', *SFN*
10–11)

If the dramatic monologue provides Duffy with a public platform for exploring issues of identity, then her love poetry surely provides her with a private one. Highly regarded for her many love poems, Duffy has, however, spoken of the difficulties of working in a genre that, perhaps more than any, depends traditionally on a division of power between lover and beloved, male and female. Perhaps because of this, with few exceptions, her love poems deal with unnamed and ungendered voices, and rarely are they explicit in their negotiation of the beloved's body. In order to explore the relationship between self and other in a form which typically places the woman as desired other, Duffy's poems explore new ways of negotiating the relationship between the subject and object of desire. She refigures heterocentric representations of desire both to affirm and problematize identity, throwing into question ideas of sameness and difference in the relationship of the lover and the beloved, and the inadequacies of language to articulate the nature of that experience.

An early poem, 'Oppenheim's Cup and Saucer' (*SP* 22), is a tightly wrought lyric which recounts a lesbian seduction. Within the context of the volume in which it appears, *Standing Female Nude* (1985), there is little explicit lesbian reference, and a 'presumed heterosexuality' permeates the volume. As such, the poem quietly invades the cultural context of heterosexuality:

OPPENHEIM'S CUP AND SAUCER

She asked me to luncheon in fur. Far from
the loud laughter of men, our secret life stirred.

I remember her eyes, the slim rope of her spine.
This is your cup, she whispered, and this is mine.

We drank the sweet hot liquid and talked dirty.
As she undressed me, her breasts were a mirror

and there were mirrors in the bed. She said Place
your legs around my neck, that's right. Yes.

The relationship between the two women takes place away from
the male world. 'Our secret life' suggests that love between
women is necessarily repressed or kept secret, but there is also
the added suggestion here – a sense of wonder or surprise late in
the poem – which also suggests that this is an initial or early
lesbian experience. Punning on the word 'stirred', Duffy is
making her only direct reference to the cup and saucer. The
ordinary act of drinking tea is juxtaposed with drinking the
liquids of each other's bodies, just as the sexual experience is one
which becomes enmeshed and encoded in the everyday. And yet
the passing of the cup between the women suggests an element
of the religious; this is communion of a secular kind, a seduction
which is both public and private, extraordinary and mundane.

Otherwise known as *Déjeuner en fourrure*, the fur-lined cup,
saucer and spoon to which Duffy's title refers is perhaps one of
the most famous and readily accessible examples of 'the
surrealist object'. First exhibited in France in 1936, *Déjeuner en
fourrure* may be seen as an archetypal dream image which has
specific reference to women and, in particular, their sexuality.
Simply in terms of its physical structure, the cup and saucer
confuse the viewer's expectation of smooth, gently rounded,
perhaps delicate, outline of china or pottery. The expectation of
these clearly defined lines is thwarted in their replacement by
the less compressed texture of the fur. The fur, which was once
part of a living creature is now integral to the inanimate
structure of the 'manmade' tea cup. In this sense, the object falls
into a kind of psychic limbo between the animate and the
inanimate, the intellectual and the emotional; and it is this
indeterminacy which provokes such a sense of shock.

Oppenheim's creation is, of course, a classic example of what

31

Freud called in his 'Three Essays on the Theory of Sexuality' the fetish object. The fetishist, the boy child who experiences the threat of castration at the same time that he sees the female genitals and 'realizes' that the female is castrated, is unable to resolve his Oedipal complex and to continue with his hetero-sexual 'development'. As Elizabeth Grosz elucidates:

> Unlike either the heterosexual or the homosexual, the fetishist wants to have his cake and eat it too: he is not prepared to 'pay' for his desire by facing the Oedipal prohibition, which gives the boy the ghastly choice – give up the mother or lose the penis – choice between his most precious object and his most precious organ.[1]

For Freud, the attachment to the sexual object which is substituted in place of the 'normal' aim, becomes detached from a particular individual and becomes instead the fetishist's sole sexual object:

> What is substituted for the sexual object is some part of the body such as the foot or hair, which is in general very inappropriate for sexual purposes, or some inanimate object which bears assignable relation to the person whom it replaces and preferably to that person's sexuality (e.g. a piece of clothing or underlinen).[2]

In his later 1927 essay 'Fetishism', Freud points out that 'fur and velvet – as has long been suspected – are a fixation of the sight of pubic hair'.[3] Interestingly, though, as Grosz points out, 'In psychoanalytic discourse, fetishism is a uniquely male perversion'. And while exploring the possibilities of female fetishism, she remains rightly ambivalent about the political ramifications of doing so:

> What relation does lesbianism have to female fetishism? In the case of the girl who has accepted her castration complex, there seems to be little or no relation. But in the case of the woman suffering from the masculinity complex it may be possible to suggest some connection. Like the fetishist, she disavows women's castration, but this castration is her own, not that of the phallic mother. And like the fetishist, she takes on a substitute for the phallus, an object outside her own body. It is this which differentiates her from the narcissist and the hysteric, both of whom phallicize or fetishize their *own* bodies, and not really preserving the fetishistic structure of the displacement of phallic value from the mother's body to an object outside one's self. By contrast the masculine woman takes an

external love-object – another woman – and through this love-object is able to function as if she *has*, rather than *is*, the phallus. As with the fetishist, this implies a splitting of the ego: it is this which inclines her to feminism itself, insofar as feminism, like any oppositional political movement, involves a disavowal of social reality so that change becomes conceivable and possible.[4]

In what way, then, must we read Duffy's appropriation of the fetish as a symbol of lesbian desire? In a recent interview, Oppenheim has spoken of the fact that it was André Breton who actually named the piece,

> playing on associations with queer sexuality in Manet's *Déjeuner sur l'herbe* and Sacher-Masoch's *Venus en fourrures*. The word-games of critics, the power struggles of men! So part of its scandalous appeal was not invented by me. It was a fluke. I had been making bits of fur covered jewellery to make a little money in 1936. I showed a piece to Picasso and Dora Maar and they joked that anything could be covered in fur – the chairs, the door. I added the cups and saucers on the table. I was thinking only of the contrast of material textures.[5]

Breton's naming of Oppenheim's object raises some interesting questions about Duffy's use of it. Sacher-Masoch's *Venus in Furs* charts the decline of a relationship between a man and a woman. In this proto-sadomasochistic text it is as much the power between men and women as aberrant sexuality which is being explored. At the beginning of the novel the narrator falls asleep beside the fire reading Hegel, and dreams of a woman who wears dark furs. The woman from the dream corresponds to a painting which he sees at his friend Severin's house of a naked woman in dark furs with a whip, who has at her feet a man who lies in front of her like a slave. Beside this picture is a copy of Titian's *Venus with the Mirror*. Severin, the novel's hero, whose diary forms the bulk of the narrative, explains the picture as

> a symbol of the tyranny and cruelty that constitute woman's essence and her beauty...The picture as it now exists, is a bitter satire on our love. Venus in this abstract North, in this icy Christian world, has to creep into huge black furs so as not to catch cold.[6]

The domination of Severin by his 'mistress' Wanda becomes increasingly excruciating as his narrative unfolds. By the end of the novel, having lost his lover's affections, Severin points out that the moral of his story is that woman, as nature has created her, and as man at present is educating her, is man's enemy. She can only be his slave or his despot, but never his companion. This she can become only when she has the same rights as he and is his equal in education and work.[7]

Manet's painting *Le Déjeuner sur l'herbe* (1863) also caused a scandal when it was first exhibited for showing two dressed males picnicking beside a naked woman. The naked woman, Manet's favourite model Victorine Meurend (whom he had also, interestingly, painted cross-dressed as a toreador) sits side-on gazing thoughtfully and directly out at the viewer. Perhaps even more interesting, though, is the correspondence between Manet's painting and *Venus with the Mirror*, the Titian cited by Sacher-Masoch early in his novel, which becomes the model for the Venus in furs in his painting. In the painting, anxiety concerning the representation of the woman's genitals becomes displaced onto the covering of fur and velvet which she wears draped around her hips. And although images of Venus gazing in a mirror are part of a tradition in Western painting, clearly also these paintings are concerned with a questioning of identity, and the relationship between self and otherness, between artist and model, painter and painted within the frame of the canvas as a whole.[8]

There is obviously a strong subtext of anxiety about the nudity and the female genitals being played out in the naming of the fur cup and saucer – and Oppenheim's *Déjeuner en fourrure* points simultaneously to the covering (through its title and the history of association behind it) and uncovering and over-determining of the pubic hair in the image of the cup and saucer itself. Whatever Oppenheim's motives were for the creation of the fur cup and saucer (and interestingly the piece now exhibited in the Museum of Modern Art in New York is simply titled *Object*), in her naming of the poem Duffy is reclaiming it as Oppenheim's while also referring to its past history. *Déjeuner en foururre* may be read not simply as an image of female sexuality, but also as a piece which through its title is linked to ideas of power relations between men and women (it is no accident after all that the narrator of *Venus in Furs* is reading Hegel).

Where then does this leave us when we find that Oppenheim was as famous in her day for her role as Man Ray's photographic model as she was for her own surreal creations? In one particular photograph of Oppenheim which originated as a part of a series, the naked Oppenheim takes on the (albeit melodramatically staged) pose of androgynous object. The surrealist obsession with androgyny is evident in her ambiguously portrayed sexuality – her breasts hidden by the wheel of the printing press, her fashionably cropped hair swept away from her face, she is masculinized by the play of shadows which cleverly reconstruct her musculature. In particular we find that her genitals have been partially covered by the wheel of the printing press by which she stands, the press's handle having been grotesquely and mischievously placed so as to reconstruct a semi-erect steel phallus.

Returning to the poem and the title, it is perhaps easier now to read the title 'Oppenheim's Cup and Saucer' as an attempt not only to rethink the image of the fur cup and saucer, but to reposition Oppenheim as the creator of the object, and to rethink her own particular dilemmas as a woman in the male-dominated surrealist movement – a process which implicitly also asks us to examine and recognize Duffy's own status as a woman writer in the 1980s. Oppenheim states in an interview:

> I believe that men, since creating Patriarchy, that is since the devaluation of the female, projected that femininity inherent in themselves, which is regarded as being inferior, onto women. This means for the women that they have had to live their own femininity plus the femininity projected onto themselves by males...[9]

Like Oppenheim, Duffy's interest in the object in the poem dramatizes an anxiety concerning the representation of the feminine. In 'Oppenheim's Cup and Saucer' Duffy places the female genitals as the central if covert image of the poem, and yet as a whole the poem maintains a certain ambivalence towards biological difference, a point which the language of the poem with its moments of phonetic sameness and semantic difference reiterates.

As a poem which is so obviously about coupling (that is the physical union of two separate bodies) and perhaps even punning on the word cup, the form of 'Oppenheim's Cup and Saucer' ideally reflects and connotes duality. Constructed in four couplets the language is perhaps deceptively simple and

35

apparently conversational in tone, but if closely examined reveals itself to be quite densely alliterative, resounding with the echoes of vowels and consonants, internal rhymes and half-rhymes, even with a full rhyme in the second couplet. Duffy's use of alliteration is closely aligned to the poem's assertion and exploration of sexual sameness. In the first line, 'She asked me to luncheon in fur. Far from', there is a rapid shift in the vowel sounds, culminating in the density of three successive consonants combined with three different vowels sounds. It would not be inappropriate to suggest that the pattern of 'fur / far / from' alerts the reader to questions of difference in visual as well as semantic power terms, and, by implication, of sexual sameness and difference. In the second line of this first couplet the alliteration used is perhaps of a more conventional nature, still echoing the 's', 'l' and 'm' from the first line. In the second couplet, however, the use of the rhyme within a sentence structure, although alliterative (slim, rope, spine), draws less attention to difference; rather it emphasizes an idea of sameness (spine, mine).

The eroticism of the poem is based on a seduction, a process in which power shifts and role play are inevitable, and yet in this seduction Duffy treads a path which is not in any way open to patriarchal judgements and stereotyping of lesbian sexuality. The power of seduction is revelled in and there is a general acknowledgement of the erotic nature of power, and yet, despite this, the eroticism in Duffy's poem is rooted in the speaker's recognition of her physical sameness with her seducer, and a realization and appreciation of her own physical identity, and, concurrently perhaps, her own sexual power. The central speaking voice of the poem is in the act of describing the woman with whom she is about to make love, and in doing this Duffy uses the image of mirrors in several complex ways. The lines 'her breasts were a mirror / and there were mirrors in the bed' are the only physical indication that this will be an experience of purely female eroticism. 'Mirrors in the bed' conjures an image of a couple viewing themselves in the act of love, eroticizing their act by objectifying it; but it also suggests that, undressed with her lover, the speaker of the poem sees her lover as likened reflection of her own visible physical self – 'her breasts were a mirror' – as well as the unseen genitals.

This preoccupation with sameness and difference is a strand which runs throughout Duffy's work. In 'Warming Her Pearls' (*SP* 60–1), an early dramatic monologue in which a maid tends her mistress, wearing her pearls in order to warm them before the mistress dresses, the model of femininity which the beloved offers is complicated by relations of class:

> I dust her shoulders with a rabbit's foot,
> watch the soft blush seep through her skin
> like an indolent sigh. In her looking-glass
> my red lips part as though I want to speak.

> Full moon. Her carriage brings her home. I see
> her every movement in my head... Undressing,
> taking off her jewels, her slim hand reaching
> for the case, slipping naked into bed, the way

> she always does... And I lie here awake,
> knowing the pearls are cooling even now
> in the room where my mistress sleeps. All night
> I feel their absence and I burn.

The distinction between self and other is here clearly demarcated: while the maid can look at her mistress, and shares the pearls, identification can never be complete because of the difference in their situations. Desire, here, for the maid, is as much a desire to become the beloved as it is to have her.

In a recent, uncollected poem 'Twins'[10], a relationship between twin sisters, or a lesbian couple (the poem is deliberately ambiguous) is examined in terms of women's relationship to the feminine and the maternal. Its slightly sinister current arises from its possible allusions to the 'Silent Twins' about whom a documentary was made in the early 1990s, who spoke an invented language known only to themselves. The poem also recalls Hollywood films which feature sisters or twins as a way of dramatizing 'good' and 'bad' models of femininity. In her reading of women in Hollywood film, Jeanine Basinger identifies four films from the 1940s: *A Stolen Life* (1946), starring Bette Davis, *Here Come the Waves*, with Betty Hutton, *Dark Mirror* (1946), starring Olivia De Havilland, and *Cobra Woman* (1944) with Maria Montez, in which sets of female twins, each played by one actress, are central.

37

Although bad selves frequently seem to be having all the fun – and also all the good clothes – the good selves survive in the end to show everyone how women ought to behave. At the same time, obviously, they allow women a peek at the fun of misbehaving, so that while accomplishing the primary purpose of the cautionary tale, they also provide that unintentionally liberating release that is built into the women's film.[11]

Of these films, two seem especially pertinent: *Dark Mirror* with its opening scene which focuses on a mirror shattered by a bullet hole, its multiple shots of the twins gazing into mirrors, its confusions between which twin is actually which; and *A Stolen Life*, to which Jackie Kay specifically refers in her long narrative poem 'The Adoption Papers':

> Maybe it's really Bette Davis I want
> to be the good twin or even better the bad
> one or a nanny who drowns a baby in a bath.[12]

But, whereas in her poem Kay is drawing attention to notions of identity based on cultural markers such as colour of the skin, and showing that the importance of establishing female role models is one which is not dependent only on 'racial' origin, Duffy's 'Twins' questions what it means to have a model of femininity. Duffy's poem, with its undercurrent of eroticism, which vacillates between nurture and control, is suffused with a sense of competition which yearns both to establish and deny difference:

TWINS

And another thing – don't say we're the same
when you're unwell and I play nurse, pour camomile
tea, poor baby. Or you put down a winning word
that I don't know and I have to look it up
in our *OED*. I love our eyes, our lips,
but not that dark red gloss and not
when you put it on to go out and smile at the friend.

Identical. But not when you haven't pierced
your ears. Not when you start to bleed
two days before, or you pull on jeans
when I want us to wear a skirt. I brush
your hair in the mirror and make you watch,
the mole on your shoulder fuzzy under my thumb.
I feel myself coming down with the dose you had,

so put me in my twin-bed and spoon our favourite soup
into my mouth. Put out the lamps. We lie on our backs
in the dark; and when I look over, your profile
does it to me again. Every time. I whisper
the words till you come across, barefooted, shy,
and say exactly the same ones back in my ear, same
ones back in my ear. Your synonymous breath.

Central to this portrayal of the two women is their relationship
to language, both written (the reference to the game of Scrabble
and the *OED*) and spoken. Like 'Oppenheim's Cup and Saucer',
the poem is concerned with the positioning of the self before the
mirror (one twin making the other twin watch as her hair is
brushed); there is a transferring of liquids into the body (the
camomile tea, the soup); but this time difference is desired and
explored until the moment of speech when difference is elided.

The preoccupation with the double arises more prominently
in two other of Duffy's later poems, '2' (*PMP* 10), in which a
young girl is assaulted by twin girls ('And when I ran / they
chased me, yanking me back by the hair;/ and what they did to
me then they did to me twice'), and 'Twinned' (*PMP* 30), which
begins:

> I have been wined and dined
> in the town with which this one is twinned.
> The people were kind, I found.
>
> I have walked hand-in-hand,
> scraped two names and a heart with a stick on the sand
> in the town with which this one is twinned,
> become over-soon over-fond.
>
> And stayed in my room when it rained,
> hearing the wind,
> with love love love on my mind,
> in the town with which this one is twinned,
> and pined.[13]

Here the end rhymes reiterate the sameness of the twins, while
the half-rhymes seem to indicate the subtlety of both sameness
and difference. The twinned town is both home and not home,
the same but different: it is its very sameness which evokes the
presence of the absent city which provokes a feeling of loss.

While problematizing ideas of the muse and exploring female

identity, 'Oppenheim's Cup and Saucer' also anticipates Duffy's later preoccupations with ideas of belonging to a region or a country which in turn merge with her quest for a lost home. For Duffy the twin is both an image of the self made strange, and a home to which she can return. In 'The Uncanny' (1919) Freud had identified the uncanny – familiar made unfamiliar through repression – with the female genitals:

> It often happens that neurotic men declare that they feel there is something uncanny about the female genital organs. The *unheimlich* place, however, is the entrance to the former *Heim* of all human beings, to the place where each one of us has lived once upon a time and in the beginning. There is a joking saying that 'Love is a homesickness'; and whenever a man dreams of a place or a country and says to himself, while he is still dreaming: 'this place is familiar to me, I've been here before', we may interpret the place as being his mother's genitals or her body. In this case too, then, the *unheimlich* is what was once *heimlich*, familiar; the prefix 'un' is the token of repression.[14]

Duffy's examination of sameness and difference also represents a search for home and a utopian desire for the maternal body where there is no difference. A later poem 'Girlfriends' (*SP* 85), illustrates a desire for a return to the *heimlich* of the maternal body. In 'Girlfriends', aside from its title, only the sex of the speaker is identified directly as being female, although the frailty of the two bodies and the fact that they are both wearing nightgowns does indicate that this is a relationship between women. The poem is derived from Verlaine's poem 'Pension-naires' which appeared in his collection *Parallèlement* (1889). Again, in her reference to Verlaine, we see Duffy looking to a model of transgressive sexuality. Verlaine had previously published the lesbian poems in this collection under the pseudonym Pablo-Maria de Herlanes. Also included in the collection were various love poems to Rimbaud, and other poems which he had written during a month in prison in 1885 – a sentence he received for drunken brutality to his mother. As well as providing a model of an erotic encounter between women, it seems likely that it is the title of the book itself, which hints at her preoccupation with doubling and sameness, which also holds appeal for Duffy.

Within Duffy's poem, orgasm and the absence of a verbally

expressed language are compressed, that which cannot be expressed being displaced onto the sound of the fire engine. Interestingly it is here, and in the move from the third to the first person, that Duffy's poem differs from Verlaine's:[15]

GIRLFRIENDS

(*derived from Verlaine for John Griffith*)

That hot September night, we slept in a single bed,
naked, and on our frail bodies the sweat
cooled and renewed itself. I reached out my arms
and you, hands on my breasts, kissed me. Evening of amber.

Our nightgowns lay on the floor where you fell to your knees
and became ferocious, pressed your head to my stomach,
your mouth to the red gold, the pink shadows; except
I did not see it like this at the time, but arched

my back and squeezed water from the sultry air
with my fists. Also I remember hearing, clearly
but distantly, a siren some streets away – *de*

da de da de da – which mingled with my own
absurd cries, so that I looked up, even then,
to see my fingers counting themselves, dancing.

In the moments of orgasm the body becomes independent, removed from the self, and inexpressible. The speaker of the poem loses herself in orgasm, and again Duffy uses juxtaposition as a way of positioning the self in an in-between state.

It's perhaps most interesting to read this poem in the light of one of Duffy's most interesting comments on the process of writing. Duffy explains:

When I'm writing a poem, when any poet is, what we are often trying to do is get the sound of a non-linguistic sort of music. I can have the rhythm or a whole sound in my head and no words. And it isn't music, it isn't language, it's something in-between. It has a colour, almost a shape. So I'm not aware that I'm doing that in a poem in a hyper-conscious level; that is partly the way I speak anyway and it will just translate into the poem like that. Whatever it is I have to say, and how I say it, that is how it's coming out. It isn't a technique and because it isn't a technique I can't describe it.[16]

What Duffy does seem to be describing is a creative impulse which privileges sound over sense, and this theme of the linguistically unsayable is picked up recurrently in Duffy's work, often identified with the idea of a prelinguistic and maternal home which in her love poems is used as a refuge from the kind of alien world in which her personae unhappily live.[17] On the one hand Duffy seems to be pointing to the inadequacies of language, while on the other she seems to be looking back nostalgically to a time before language itself.

In 'Homesick' (*SM* 19), which seems to echo Freud's commentary in his essay on the uncanny – 'Love is a homesickness' – we see the desire to place the unplaceable, to recapture the prelinguistic, the country which is other, because we can never speak or reclaim it. Whereas in 'Oppenheim's Cup and Saucer' we saw Duffy offering a conjunction between the *heimlich* and the *unheimlich*, the natural and the constructed, 'Homesick' articulates fully the impossible desire to return to the maternal body:

HOMESICK

When we love, when we tell ourselves we do,
we are pining for first love, somewhen,
before we thought of wanting it. When we rearrange
the rooms we end up living in, we are looking
for first light, the arrangement of light,
that time, before we knew to call it light.

Or talk of music, when we say
we cannot talk of it, but play again
C major, A flat minor, we are straining
for first sound, what we heard once,
then, in lost chords, wordless languages.

What country do we come from? This one?
The one where the sun burns
when we have night? The one
the moon chills; elsewhere, possible?

Why is our love imperfect,
music only echo of itself
the light wrong?

We scratch in dust with sticks,
dying of homesickness
for when, where, what.

Duffy's nostalgia for an Imaginary identity which is equally a desire for self which is ungendered and undifferentiated is, of course, a utopian and impossible project. In 'Homesick', the act

42

of articulating the loss of that which by its nature cannot be articulated acknowledges the unobtainable nature of her desires while nevertheless deriving pleasure from the momentary recreation (both through memory, and through the act of creating a poem) of the realization of that loss. In 'Words, Wide Night' (*SP* 86) and 'Two Small Poems of Desire' (*TOC* 42), love and its expression become implicated in both self-expression and the representation of the self, 'singing / an impossible song of desire that you cannot hear'. It is song, or the representation of song – 'La lala la' – which shows, 'what it is like or what it is like in words'.

In 'Demeter', the final poem in *The World's Wife*, however, we find a different kind of love poem. This fourteen line poem, which, with its final couplet, obviously nods towards the sonnet form, brings the volume full circle, from the ingenue Little Red Cap in the first poem, to the redemptive image of the daughter, watched by the mother whose 'broken heart' is healed by her return from the underworld:

> Where I lived – winter and hard earth.
> I sat in my cold stone room
> choosing tough words, granite, flint,
>
> to break the ice. My broken heart –
> I tried that, but it skimmed,
> flat, over the frozen lake.
>
> She came from a long, long way,
> but I saw her at last, walking,
> my daughter my girl, across the fields
>
> in bare feet, bringing all spring's flowers
> to her mother's house. I swear
> the air softened and warmed as she moved,
>
> the blue sky smiling, none too soon,
> with the small shy mouth of a new moon.

The poem, through its title, focuses on the mother rather than the daughter. The Greek myth of Persephone is obliquely told, and it's interesting too, that while the poem is written in the first person, it is not strictly a dramatic monologue. While 'Little Red Cap' ends with the image of the girl who has just left the wolf, escaping, 'Out of the forest with my flowers, singing, all alone', (*WW*, 4) in this poem the return or birth of the daughter heralds spring. The image of words being chosen 'to break the ice' recalls Kafka's famous declaration that words must be the axe to break the frozen sea within us. It is as if the carapace of the dramatic monologue is relinquished in favour of a new beginning. The daughter, who is both the poet's self and other, abnegates song and the prelapsarian hankering for a time when words and music were one, in favour of a prescient silence.[18]

I began this chapter with a quotation from Duffy's 'Alphabet for Auden', and it is to this poem I would like now to return. The poem begins with the lines 'When the words have gone away / there is nothing left to say'. Duffy's desire to return to the time when both her sexual and her speaking identity are impossible seems potentially liberating but also potentially dangerous. Her nostalgia for an unremembered Imaginary identity depends only on her ability to express its absence: without language, it seems important to remember, Duffy would have no medium through which to either celebrate or denigrate. Moreover, her preoccupation with finding a safe place in which to love cannot be removed from the realities of the world in which she lives and in which she may be oppressed for expressing the full range of her sexuality. Duffy has few models for the love poem which do not reinscribe a dependent and dyadic relationship based on the fixing of roles. In the love poems I have discussed, the relationship between self and other is a complex one, premised, it might be argued, on a need simultaneously to disavow female castration, on the one hand, and to articulate loss on the other. These poems demonstrate an anxiety concerning not only female power but the representation of female subjectivity; and, perhaps paradoxically, it is this anxiety which also enables Duffy, as we have seen, to position herself in her dramatic monologues as both self and other.

4

Mean Times

Not to speak the language makes you
innocent again, invisible...

('Oslo' *MT* 32)

In a *Poetry Book Society Bulletin* in 1993, Duffy discusses the multiple resonances of the title of her fourth collection, *Mean Time*, indicating the development of both her formal and thematic preoccupations. She explains:

> The poems in *Mean Time* are about the different ways in which time brings about change or loss. In the collection, I mean to write about time. The effects of time can be mean. Mean can mean average. The events in the poems can happen to the average man or woman. The dwindling of childhood. Ageing. The distance of history. The tricks of memory and the renewal of language. The end of love. Divorce. New love. Luck. And so on. In the last book...I had begun to write more personal, autobiographical poems; and this switch from the dramatic-monologue dominated stance of earlier collections is intensified in *Mean Time*. I found it interesting that the techniques stumbled across and refined in writing 'Other Voices' helped me to pitch my own voice – for we all have several – particularly when finding language for the painful areas dealt with in the poems.[1]

The collection is framed by the positioning of three poems, 'Litany' (*SP* 95–6), 'Confession' (*MT* 15) and the final poem, 'Prayer' (*SP* 127), which is reminiscent both of Heaney's seventh Glanmore sonnet,[2] and Eliot in 'Little Gidding' when he writes 'And prayer is more / Than an order of words, the conscious occupation / Of the praying mind, or the sound of the voice praying'.[3] The effects of her Catholic upbringing have been of obvious importance, and in an interview in 1991 Duffy explains:

45

I think, now, I retain some of the motifs of all that and none of the feelings; faith, guilt, whatever. I do envy people who have a religious faith – I can recall the comfort, the sense of a safety net. I still enjoy the sensuality of aspects of the Catholic religion and a lot of the imagery.[4]

In adopting a more personal tone than her earlier books, Duffy does not, however, turn wholly away from her earlier interests.

The poem which begins the volume, 'The Captain of the 1964 *Top of the Form* Team' (*SP* 93–4) is concerned with history and memory, and elicits a nostalgia for a lost childhood, which is not so much sentimentalized as fondly recalled. As we have seen, in Duffy's monologues, there is often a slippage between the voice of the monologist and the voice of another presence which interferes or seeps into the narrative. The sex of the monologist is not immediately apparent, and it is not until the end of the first stanza that we realize that the speaker of the poem is male. The speaker of the monologue, who is remembering his childhood and the seemingly uncomplicated way it allowed him to view the world, is looking back with a desire to reclaim this simplified version of the world in which he always knew the answers: 'I want it back. The Captain. The one with all the answers. Bzz.'

The poem is an assemblage of broken sounds – fragments, in Eliot's words, to shore against ruin. The speaker's, and perhaps the poet's, nostalgia for the past is also a nostalgia for song and non-representational sound – gargling with Vimto, the playing on the comb, the whoop, the rote learning of Latin; even written representation is idealized, not as language, but as the 'pink pavements that girls chalked on' and the child's stamping of 'the pawprints of badgers and skunks in the mud'. Underwriting personal memory and history, however, are intertextual references which recall key modernist writers' attempts to deal with the relationship between the self, art and history.

In the first line we perhaps hear the early lines of Joyce's *A Portrait of the Artist as a Young Man*, as we are brought from the language of the baby to the language of the male adult: '*Do Wah Diddy Diddy, Baby Love, Oh Pretty Woman*'. These fragments, which the reader, like the child in the quiz, must guess, are presented as a seemingly random assemblage. Personal time (months and hours) are pitted against the indications of passing time in popular culture (the 'Top Ten'); and history itself in the learning of the dates of the kings and the queens, and the memorialization of an imperial past in the naming of Churchill Way and Nelson Drive. The reference to the 'humming-bird's song' perhaps recalls Lawrence's 'Humming-Bird' who lives 'in some other-world/ Primeval-dumb, far back / In that most awful stillness, that only gasped and hummed'.[5] This in turn is juxtaposed with Eliot's *The Waste Land* ('I sped down Dyke Hill, no hands, famous, learning, *dominus domine dominum*'). The speaker of Eliot's poem asks his companion, Marie, to 'hold on tight'; Duffy's monologist, however, sledges with no hands; learning mastery while learning how to (perhaps ironically) decline it. The poem ends on a pessimistic note, recalling Yeats's 'Among School Children' ('*How can we know the dancer from the dance?* Nobody') and ends with lines suggesting that all that is left for the monologist's 'thick kids' is the residue of imperialism and the persistence of capitalism: '*Name the Prime Minister of Rhodesia.* / My country. *How many florins in a pound?*'

Temporal progression in the poem is represented by the progression from stanza to stanza through word association. Thus 'snog' at the end of stanza one becomes 'No snags' at the beginning of stanza two; '*dominum*' at the end of stanza two becomes '*Dave Dee Dozy*' at the beginning of stanza three. Central to this progression of time is the subtext of difficulty between men and women – between the snag and the snog, Dave's potential mastery. Lucille Green's childhood crush on the monologist is represented in terms of fear and loss, his smile 'as wide as a child who went missing on the way home / from school'. The protagonist's wife is 'stale'; their union has produced 'thick kids'. Ostensibly there seems to be no answer and the poem seems to be as much a lament for the monologist's past as it is for a loss of the power of language and a literary tradition to which only the isolated monologist, it seems, now has recourse.

In 'Litany', which immediately follows, these themes are continued. The litany is not the Catholic litany, or the declension of Latin nouns, but a litany of cultural artifacts that represent aspiring working-class respectability – '*candlewick / bedspread three piece suite display cabinet –* / and stiff-haired wives balanced their red smiles, / passing the catalogue. *Pyrex.*' The poem, a bitter satire against the repressive culture of her upbringing, itself becomes a litany of all those things deemed unsayable in the world 'where no one had cancer, or sex, or debts, / and certainly not leukaemia, which no one could spell'. The later stream of consciousness poem 'Confession', recalls an earlier poem, 'Words of Absolution' (*SFN* 32) in which the experiences of a younger voice are juxtaposed with the Catholicism of a dying older grandmother. The voice of the earlier poem pits sexual experience against Catholic dogma and ends by asking:

> What are the four last things
> to be ever remembered? I go to my reward.
> Chastity. Piety. Modesty. Longanimity.
> How should you finish the day? After
> your night prayers what should you do?

In contrast, the later poem recalls the Catholic confessional as a way of questioning how we can confess or be redeemed if we exist outside religion:

> Just how bad have you been there's no water
> in hell merely to think of a wrong's as evil
> as doing it...*For I have sinned*...Penance
> will cleanse you like a bar of good soap so
> say the words into the musty gloom aye
> on your knees let's hear that wee voice
> recite transgression in the manner approved...*Forgive me*

'Prayer' (*SP* 127), the sonnet which ends the volume, offers, however, some kind of secular consolation: this consolation is memory.

PRAYER

> Some days, although we cannot pray, a prayer
> utters itself. So, a woman will lift
> her head from the sieve of her hands and stare
> at the minims sung by a tree, a sudden gift.

> Some nights, although we are faithless, the truth
> enters our hearts, that small familiar pain;
> then a man will stand stock-still, hearing his youth
> in the distant Latin chanting of a train.

> Pray for us now. Grade I piano scales
> console the lodger looking out across
> a Midlands town. Then dusk, and someone calls
> a child's name as though they named their loss.

Darkness outside. Inside, the radio's prayer –
Rockall. Malin. Dogger. Finisterre.

This sonnet draws together many of Duffy's preoccupations: desire, loss, the surreal image of a minim tree, nostalgia for a lost childhood, the urge to name and the absence of words with which to name. Seen together, these poems work to frame a volume which looks back on a life in the light of a failing love affair, leaving the speakers of the poems in the limbo evoked in the title poem, when the clocks have gone back, an hour has been lost, the summer (both real and metaphorical) is ending:

MEAN TIME

The clocks slid back an hour
and stole light from my life
as I walked through the wrong part of town,
mourning our love.

And, of course, unmendable rain
fell to the bleak streets
where I felt my heart gnaw
at all our mistakes.

If the darkening sky could lift
more than one hour from this day
there are words I would never have said
nor have heard you say.

But we will be dead, as we know,
beyond all light.
These are the shortened days
and the endless nights.

(SP 126)

Within this limbo, bodies appear and disappear; nothing seems real. In 'Never Go Back' (*MT* 30–1), 'You follow your shadow / through the house, discover objects held/ in the hands can fill a room with pain'; in 'The Grammar of Light' (*SP* 113), in which the poet looks to objects rather than to the inadequate language we have for the naming of objects, 'all faces blur / to dreams of themselves held in the eyes'. And although we are presented with a realist world of rain and rented rooms, of adultery, businessmen and UB40s, it is a world that slips in and out of perception, in and out of memory, language, dreams. In 'Steam' (*MT* 36), the lover and the beloved's body, 'a nude pose in soft pencil / behind tissue paper', appear and disappear, until the shock at the end of the poem when the lover stretches out to find 'the real thing, / shockingly there, / not a ghost at all'.

*

Duffy's veering from the public to the private, between time and place, estrangement and belonging, the realist and the modernist, are not, of course, a veering between the polarized positions they might at first seem. Rather, they illustrate a continuing exploration of personal history in time and place, and of identity and difference – in particular in the moment when sexual difference is first experienced. As we have seen, Duffy's use of the dramatic monologue allows a socialization of the self, enabled by the projected fantastic self who carries utterance without fear of censorship. In doing this it offers a double release: not only does it provide a way of negotiating the construction of subjectivity in a poem, but for the poet, safely disassociated from the persona who speaks, it offers another way of projecting a fantasy not obviously or directly emanating from her own life experience. Perhaps most interestingly, it signals an uneasiness about presenting a version of the self which is readily identifiable with the poet, while simultaneously, as a form of protection of the 'authentic' self, cleverly offering, in the process, a critique of those very notions of authenticity it seems in some way to promote.

In her love poems, Duffy experiments with both gendered and ungendered voices in order to renegotiate the boundary between self and other, lover and beloved. Often the speaking of desire is an articulation of loss, as is, for Duffy, any act of naming, whether it be the 'inconsolable vowels in the next room', or the 'adjectives' or 'abstract nouns'. Only 'In moments of grace', she writes, 'we were verbs, the secret of poems' ('Moments of Grace', SP 111–12). In her desire to return to an Imaginary state, Duffy values experience over the failure of telling that experience. Yet, as if to compensate for this, her poems set out to memorialize the irrecoverable. In a recent interview she has spoken of 'The beginning of the poem' as being 'always a moment of tiny revelation...a new way of seeing something, which almost simultaneously attracts language to it – and then the impulse is to catch that with pen and paper'. The poem is then worked until it 'seems to have assumed the same shape as the original revelation'.[6] For while enacting loss, both the writing and the reading of the poem seem to allow us, Duffy suggests, a way to re-experience that which will otherwise always escape us. 'What is the language using us for?' asks W. S. Graham. Duffy's work is both continuous reiteration of and answer to this question.

Notes

PROLOGUE

1. *The New Poetry*, ed. Michael Hulse, David Kennedy and David Morley (Newcastle: Bloodaxe, 1993), 16.
2. Interview with Andrew McAllister, *Bête Noire*, 6 (Winter 1988), 71.

CHAPTER 1. BEGINNINGS

1. *Surrealist Poetry in English*, edited with an introduction by Edward B. Germain (Harmondsworth: Penguin, 1978).
2. Like surrealism, Cixous's philosophy is in many ways an aesthetic of gendered oppositions, setting itself up against the already evidenced binarisms of patriarchal culture, but nevertheless using them to demonstrate the silenced position of the feminine in culture and society. Surrealism, in its mystification and mythologizing of the feminine, reinforces binary thought through a juxtaposition which never lets boundaries blur, but works by bifurcating between them, establishing difference by constructing clashes of yoked-together otherness. Cixous's aesthetic, however, attempts to do away with binary divisions.
3. Cited in Rob Jackaman, *The Course of English Surrealist Poetry since the 1930s* (Lewiston: Emellon Press, 1989), 247.
4. *Poetry Review*, vol. 73, no. 4 (January, 1984), 37.
5. That is presuming that the poem entered for the competition was identical, or at least very similar, to the poem of the same title which later appeared in *Standing Female Nude* (1985).
6. *Collected Works*, vol. 1, trans. Victor Corti (London: Calder and Boyars, 1968), 69–70.
7. Carol Ann Duffy, interview with Andrew McAllister, *Bête Noire*, 6 (Winter 1988), 75–6.
8. *Tonight at Noon* (London: Rapp and Whiting, 1968), 80.

9. John Golding, 'Cubism', in *Concepts of Modern Art*, revised and enlarged edition, ed. Nikos Stangos (London: Thames and Hudson, 1981), 57.

CHAPTER 2. MASQUERADES

1. Robert Langbaum, *The Poetry of Experience* (New York: Norton, 1963), 79.
2. Isobel Armstrong, *Victorian Poetry: Poetry, Poetics and Politics* (London: Routledge, 1993), 325.
3. '"The Intolerable Wrestle with Words": the Poetry of Carol Ann Duffy', *Bête Noire*, 6 (Winter 1988), 79.
4. 'Whispers of Immortality', *Collected Poems 1909–1962* (London: Faber, 1974), 55–6.
5. I am thinking particularly of the following lines:
   My mind is a fairground
   Noise-Gaiety-Bright
   colours, at the back
   THE VAMPIRES CAVE
   huge bats with horrible
   wings like old umbrellas
   (but the vampires are really fruitbats
   and live mostly on old peaches the punters won't buy)
   And the FUN HOUSE with the beautiful dark-eyed madonna
   who smiles at me but is married to someone else
   And pimply girls in cowboy hats
   THE CISCO KID emerge and lascivious compressed air
                              blows up their skirts
   (sometimes they cross this part three or four times)
   Beautiful little girls of 12 or 13 in enormous sunglasses
   With beautiful tight little arses
   (like two plums in a wet paper bag)
   and firm little tits like toffee apples 6d.
   she smiles at me sexily (holding her mother's
   arm) her mouth bursting with little even teeth
   knowing I want to have her and can't
   ('*Don't be a burke, you'd get your collar felt*')
   And always in my mind echoes of false promises:
       YOU CAN PICK WHAT YOU LIKE.
6. *Contemporary Poetry and Postmodernism: Dialogue and Estrangement* (London: Macmillan, 1996), 96–7.
7. Interview with Jane Stabler, *Verse*, vol. 8, no. 2 (Summer 1991), 127.
8. *Feminism and Poetry: Language, Identity and Experience* (London:

Pandora, 1987), 97–178.
9. *Feminism and Poetry*, 142–3.
10. Judith Butler, *Gender Trouble: Feminism and the Subversion of Identity* (London: Routledge, 1990), 52.
11. Reprinted in *Formations of Fantasy*, ed. Victor Burgin, with James Donald and Cora Kaplan (London: Routledge, 1986), 38.
12. *New Introductory Lectures on Psychoanalysis*, vol. 2, Penguin Freud Library (Harmondsworth: Penguin, 1991), 166–7.
13. *Speculum of the Other Woman* (Ithaca, NY: Cornell University Press, 1985), 115.
14. Interview with Andrew McAllister, *Bête Noire*, 6 (Winter 1988), 72.
15. *Speculum of the Other Woman*, 116.
16. *Anne Sexton: A Self-Portrait in Letters*, ed. Linda Gray Sexton and Lois Ames, with a new foreword by Linda Gray Sexton (Houghton Mifflin Company: Boston, New York and London, 1991), 362.
17. Interview with Christina Patterson, *The Independent: The Weekend Review* (2nd October 1999).
18. Cited by Jack Zipes, 'A Second gaze at Red Riding Hood's Trials and Tribulations' in *Don't Bet on the Prince* ed Jack Zipes (Aldershot and New York: Gower, 1986), p. 230.
19. The phrase 'the cave of words', recalls Irigaray's reading of Plato in *Speculum of the Other Woman*, 243–364.

CHAPTER 3.   LOVE POEMS: A PLACE CALLED HOME

1. Elizabeth Grosz, *Space, Time, Perversion* (London: Routledge, 1995), 144.
2. 'Three Essays on the Theory of Sexuality', in *On Sexuality: Three Essays on the Theory of Sexuality and Other Works*, trans. under editorship of James Strachey, compiled and edited by Angela Richards, Penguin Freud Library, vol. 7 (Harmondsworth: Penguin, 1991), 65–6.
3. 'Three Essays on the Theory of Sexuality', 354.
4. *Space, Time, Perversion*, 153.
5. Robert J. Belton, 'Androgyny: Interview with Meret Oppenheim', in *Surrealism and Women*, ed. Mary Ann Caws, Rudolf Kuenzli and Gwen Raaberg (Cambridge, MA, and London, England: MIT Press, 1991), 68.
6. Leopold von Sacher-Masoch, *Venus in Furs and Letters of Leopold von Sacher-Masoch and Emilie Mataja*, trans. Uwe Moeller and Laura Lindgren, foreword by Sylvere Lotringer (New York: Blast Books, 1989), 61.
7. von Sacher-Masoch, *Venus in Furs*, 210.

8. Manet's painting, *Olympia*, painted in the same year as his *Déjeuner sur l'herbe*, which evolves from his *Copy of Titian's Venus of Urbino*, further dramatizes this preoccupation with the female sex organs. Here, the proud figure of a naked woman on the left of the painting guards her privacy with a well-placed hand. Her sexuality is displaced onto the right side of the painting by a representation of flowers, the black woman and the black cat.
9. Rozsika Parker and Griselda Pollock, *Old Mistresses: Women, Art and Ideology* (London: Pandora, 1987), 144.
10. *Sunday Times*, 'Books' section (5th September 1993), 5.
11. *A Woman's View: How Hollywood Spoke to Women 1930–1960* (London: Chatto, 1993), 84.
12. *The Adoption Papers* (Newcastle: Bloodaxe, 1991), 26.
13. See also 'The Kray Sisters' (*WW*, 63–65) and 'Elvis's Twin Sister' (*WW*, 66–67).
14. Penguin Freud Library, vol. 14 (Harmondsworth: Penguin, 1990), 368.
15. Verlaine, *Œuvres poètiques complètes* (Paris: Gallimard, 1962), 486–7. Text annotated by Y.-G. Le Dantec, revised edition by Jacques Borel:

> L'une avait quinze ans, l'autre en avait seize;
> Toutes deux dormaient dans la même chambre.
> C'était par un soir très lourd de septembre:
> Frêles, des yeux bleus, des rougeurs de fraise.
>
> Chacune a quitté, pour se mettre à l'aise,
> La fine chemise au frais parfum d'ambre.
> La plus jeune étend les bras, et se cambre,
> Et sa sœur, les mains sur ses seins, la baise,
>
> Puis tombe à genoux, puis devient farouche
> Et tumultueuse et folle, et sa bouche
> Plonge sous l'or blond, dans les ombres grises;
>
> Et l'enfant, pendant ce temps-là, recense
> Sur ses doigts mignons des valses promises,
> Et, rose, sourit avec innocence.

16. Interview with Andrew McAllister, *Bête Noire*, 6 (Winter, 1988), 75.
17. Lacan's theory, which I discuss very briefly in the preceding chapter, was developed interestingly in 1936, the year of the surrealist exhibition in which *Déjeuner en fourrure* was first shown.
18. For an interesting discussion of music and the unsayable see Sally Kilmister, 'Listen in to the Past: Myth Music and the Unsayable' in *Poetry Wales*, vol. 32, no. 2 (October 1996), 12–16. See also Rita Dove's *Mother Love* (New York: Norton, 1995) a book-length sequence which explores the Demeter/Persephone myth.

CHAPTER 4. MEAN TIMES

1. Reprinted from the *Poetry Society Bulletin*, Summer 1993, in *Poetry Review*, vol. 84, no. 1 (Spring 1994), 111.
2. *New and Selected Poems 1966–1987* (London: Faber, 1990), 115.
3. *Collected Poems 1909–1962* (London: Faber, 1974), 215.
4. Interview with Jane Stabler, *Verse*, vol. 8, no. 2 (Summer 1991), 124.
5. D. H. Lawrence, *Selected Poetry*, selected and introduced by Keith Sagar, revised edition (Harmondsworth: Penguin, 1986), 85.
6. Interview with Christina Patterson, *The Independent: The Weekend Review* (2nd October, 1999).

Select Bibliography

WORKS BY CAROL ANN DUFFY

Fleshweathercock (Walton-on-Thames: Outposts Press, 1974).
Beauty and the Beast (Liverpool: Glasshouse Press, 1977). Pamphlet, with Adrian Henri.
Fifth Last Song (Liverpool: Headland, 1982).
Thrown Voices (London: Turret Books, 1983). Pamphlet.
Standing Female Nude (London: Anvil, 1985).
Selling Manhattan (London: Anvil, 1987).
The Other Country (London: Anvil, 1990).
William and the Ex-Prime Minister (London: Anvil, 1992). Pamphlet.
Mean Time (London: Anvil, 1993).
Selected Poems (Harmondsworth: Penguin, 1944).
Grimm Tales, adapted by Carol Ann Duffy, dramatized by Tim Supple (London: Faber, 1996).
More Grimm Tales, adapted by Carol Ann Duffy, dramatized by Tim Supple (London: Faber 1997).
The Pamphlet (London: Anvil, 1998).
The World's Wife (London: Picador, 1999).
Rumplestiltskin and Other Grimm Tales, with Markete Prachaticka (London: Faber, 1999).
Meeting Midnight (London: Faber, 1999). Poems for children.
Five Finger-Piglets with Brian Patten, Roger McGough, Jackie Kay, Gareth Owen and Peter Bailey (Basingstoke: Macmillan, 1999).
The Oldest Girl in the World (London: Faber, 2000). Poems for children.

Edited Works

I Wouldn't Thank You for a Valentine (London: Viking, 1992; Penguin, 1995).
Anvil New Poets 2 (London: Anvil, 1994).
Stopping for Death (Harmondsworth: Penguin, 1996).

Anvil New Poets (London: Anvil, 1996).
Time's Tidings: Greeting the Twenty-First Century (London: Anvil, 1999).
Hand in Hand: An Anthology of Love Poems (London: Picador, 2001).

CRITICAL STUDIES/INTERVIEWS

Bertram, Vicki, *Gendering Poetry: Contemporary women and men poets* (Pandora, 2005).
Bentley, Vicci, interview with Carol Ann Duffy, *Magma* 3 (Winter 1994), 17–24.
Brittan, Simon, 'Language and Structure in the Poetry of Carol Ann Duffy', *Thumbscrew*, 1 (Winter 1994/5), 58–64.
Broom, Sarah, *Contemporary British and Irish Poetry: An Introduction* (Palgrave Macmillan, 2005).
Cox, Marion and Swan, Robert (eds.), *Selected Poems of Carol Ann Duffy*, York Notes Advanced Series (Longman, 2005).
Crawford, Robert, *Identifying Poets: Self and Territory in Twentieth-Century Poetry* (Edinburgh: Edinburgh University Press, 1993).
Day, Gary, and Brian Docherty (eds.), *British Poetry from the 1950s to the 1990s: Politics and Art* (Basingstoke: Macmillan, 1997).
Danette Dimarco, 'Exposing Nude Art: Carol Ann Duffy's response to Robert Browning', *Mosaic: A Journal for the Interdisciplinary Study of Literature* 31.3 (September 1998).
Gregson, Ian, *Poetry and Postmodernism: Dialogue and Estrangement* (Basingstoke: Macmillan, 1996).
Kennedy, David, *New Relations: The Refashioning of British Poetry* (Bridgend: Seren, 1996).
Kinnahan, Linda, '"Look for the Doing Words": Carol Ann Duffy and Questions of Convention', in *Contemporary British Poetry: Essays in Theory and Criticism*, eds. James Acheson and Romana Huk (New York: State University of New York Press, 1996), 245–68.
———, '"Now I am Alien": Immigration and the Discourse of Nation in the Poetry of Carol Ann Duffy' in *Contemporary Women's Poetry: Reading/Writing/Practice* eds. Alison Mark and Deryn Rees-Jones (Basingstoke: Macmillan, 2000), 208–25.
McAllister, Andrew, interview with Carol Ann Duffy, *Bête Noire*, 6 (Winter 1988), 69–77.
Michelis, Angelica and Rowland, Anthony (eds.), *Choosing Tough Words: The Poetry of Carol Ann Duffy* (Manchester: Manchester University Press, 2003).
Patterson, Christina, 'Carol Ann Duffy': Street-wise heroines at home'. Interview in *The Independent: The Weekend Review*, 2nd October, 1999.

Pinnington, David, *Carol Ann Duffy and Simon Armitage and Pre-1914 Poetry*, York Notes Series (Longman, 2003).

Radstone, Susannah, 'Remembering Medea: The Uses of Nostalgia', *Critical Quarterly*, vol. 35, no. 3 (1993), 54–63.

Rees-Jones, Deryn, *Consorting with Angels: Essays on Modern Women Poets* (Bloodaxe, 2005). Includes discussion of Duffy's poems in *The World's Wife* in a chapter on myth, fairytale and feminism, 158–64.

Robinson, Alan, *Instabilities in Contemporary British Poetry* (Basingstoke: Macmillan, 1988).

Stabler, Jane, interview with Carol Ann Duffy, *Verse*, vol. 8, no. 2 (Summer 1991), 124–8.

Thomas, Jane, E., ' "The Intolerable Wrestle with Words": The Poetry of Carol Ann Duffy', *Bête Noire*, 6 (Winter 1988), 78–88.

Viner, Katherine, 'MetreMaid'. Interview/article in *The Guardian: Weekend*, 25th September, 1999.

Useful websites

An updated biography/bibliography can be accessed on the web through 'The Knitting Circle' at http://www.sbu.ac.uk/~stafflag/carolannduffy.html

sheerpoetry.co.uk. Billed as resources on poetry by the poets themselves, this site works by subscription only.

Manuscript material dating from 1985–1999 can be found at Emory University, including notebooks and other drafts of poems from *Standing Female Nude, Selling Manhattan, The Other Country, Mean Time* and *The World's Wife*.

Index

Recent and Forthcoming Titles in the New Series of

WRITERS AND THEIR WORK

"...this series promises to outshine its own previously high reputation."
Times Higher Education Supplement

"...will build into a fine multi-volume critical encyclopaedia of English literature."
Library Review & Reference Review

"...Excellent, informative, readable, and recommended."
NATE News

"written by outstanding contemporary critics, whose expertise is flavoured by unashamed enthusiasm for their subjects and the series' diverse aspirations."
Times Educational Supplement

"A useful and timely addition to the ranks of the lit crit and reviews genre. Written in an accessible and authoritative style."
Library Association Record

WRITERS AND THEIR WORK

RECENT & FORTHCOMING TITLES

Title	Author
Chinua Achebe	Nahem Yousaf
Peter Ackroyd	Susana Onega
Fleur Adcock	Janet Wilson
Kingsley Amis	Richard Bradford
Anglo-Saxon Verse	Graham Holderness
Antony and Cleopatra 2/e	Ken Parker
Matthew Arnold	Kate Campbell
As You Like It	Penny Gay
Margaret Atwood	Marion Wynne-Davies
W. H. Auden	Stan Smith
Jane Austen	Robert Miles
Alan Ayckbourn	Michael Holt
J. G. Ballard	Michel Delville
Pat Barker	Sharon Monteith
Djuna Barnes	Deborah Parsons
Julian Barnes	Matthew Pateman
Samuel Beckett	Sinead Mooney
Aphra Behn 2/e	S. J. Wiseman
John Betjeman	Dennis Brown
William Blake	Steven Vine
Edward Bond	Michael Mangan
Anne Brontë	Betty Jay
Emily Brontë	Stevie Davies
Robert Browning	John Woolford
Robert Burns	Gerard Carruthers
A. S. Byatt	Richard Todd
Byron	Drummond Bone
Caroline Drama	Julie Sanders
Angela Carter 2/e	Lorna Sage
Geoffrey Chaucer	Steve Ellis
Children's Literature	Kimberley Reynolds
Caryl Churchill 3/e	Elaine Aston
John Clare	John Lucas
Arthur Hugh Clough	John Schad
S. T. Coleridge	Stephen Bygrave
Joseph Conrad	Cedric Watts
Coriolanus	Anita Pacheco
Stephen Crane	Kevin Hayes
Crime Fiction	Martin Priestman
Anita Desai	Elaine Ho
Shashi Deshpande	Armrita Bhalla
Charles Dickens	Rod Mengham
John Donne	Stevie Davies
Margaret Drabble	Glenda Leeming
John Dryden	David Hopkins
Douglas Dunn	David Kennedy
Early Modern Sonneteers	Michael Spiller
George Eliot	Josephine McDonagh
T. S. Eliot	Colin MacCabe
English Translators of Homer	Simeon Underwood
J. G. Farrell	John McLeod

RECENT & FORTHCOMING TITLES

Title   Author

Title	Author
Henry Fielding	Jenny Uglow
Veronica Forrest-Thomson – Language Poetry	Alison Mark
E. M. Forster	Nicholas Royle
John Fowles	William Stephenson
Brian Friel	Geraldine Higgins
Athol Fugard	Dennis Walder
Elizabeth Gaskell	Kate Flint
The Gawain-Poet	John Burrow
The Georgian Poets	Rennie Parker
William Golding 2/e	Kevin McCurron
Graham Greene	Peter Mudford
Neil M. Gunn	J. B. Pick
Ivor Gurney	John Lucas
Hamlet 2/e	Ann Thompson & Neil Taylor
Thomas Hardy 2/e	Peter Widdowson
Tony Harrison	Joe Kelleher
William Hazlitt	J. B. Priestley; R. L. Brett (intro. by Michael Foot)
Seamus Heaney 3/e	Andrew Murphy
Henry IV	Laurence Lerner
George Herbert	T.S. Eliot (intro. by Peter Porter)
Geoffrey Hill	Andrew Roberts
Gerard Manley Hopkins	Daniel Brown
Ted Hughes	Susan Bassnett
Henrik Ibsen 2/e	Sally Ledger
The Imagist Poets	Andrew Thacker
Kazuo Ishiguro 2/e	Cynthia Wong
Henry James – The Later Writing	Barbara Hardy
James Joyce 2/e	Steven Connor
Julius Caesar	Mary Hamer
Franz Kafka	Michael Wood
John Keats	Kelvin Everest
James Kelman	Gustav Klaus
Rudyard Kipling	Jan Montefiore
Hanif Kureishi	Ruvani Ranasinha
Samuel Johnson	Liz Bellamy
William Langland: Piers Plowman	Claire Marshall
King Lear	Terence Hawkes
Philip Larkin 2/e	Laurence Lerner
D. H. Lawrence	Linda Ruth Williams
Vernon Lee	Sandeep Kandola
Doris Lessing	Elizabeth Maslen
C. S. Lewis	William Gray
Wyndham Lewis and Modernism	Andrzej Gasiorek
David Lodge	Bernard Bergonzi
Macbeth	Kate McLuskie
Norman MacCaig	Alasdair Macrae
Louis MacNeice & Poetry of 1930s	Richard D. Brown
Katherine Mansfield	Andrew Bennett
Christopher Marlowe	Thomas Healy
Andrew Marvell	Annabel Patterson
Ian McEwan 2/e	Kiernan Ryan
Measure for Measure	Kate Chedgzoy

Title	Author
The Merchant of Venice	Warren Chernaik
Middleton and His Collaborators	Hutchings & Bromham
A Midsummer Night's Dream	Helen Hackett
John Milton	Nigel Smith
Alice Munro	Ailsa Cox
Vladimir Nabokov	Neil Cornwell
V. S. Naipaul	Suman Gupta
New Woman Writers	Marion Shaw/Lyssa Randolph
Grace Nichols	Sarah Lawson-Welsh
Edna O'Brien	Amanda Greenwood
Flann O'Brien	Joe Brooker
Ben Okri	Robert Fraser
George Orwell	Douglas Kerr
Othello	Emma Smith
Walter Pater	Laurel Brake
Brian Patten	Linda Cookson
Caryl Phillips	Helen Thomas
Harold Pinter	Mark Batty
Sylvia Plath 2/e	Elisabeth Bronfen
Pope Amongst the Satirists	Brean Hammond
Pre-Romantic Poetry	Vincent Quinn
Revenge Tragedies of the Renaissance	Janet Clare
Jean Rhys 2/e	Helen Carr
Richard II	Margaret Healy
Richard III	Edward Burns
Dorothy Richardson	Carol Watts
John Wilmot, Earl of Rochester	Germaine Greer
Romeo and Juliet	Sasha Roberts
Christina Rossetti	Kathryn Burlinson
Salman Rushdie 2/e	Damian Grant
Paul Scott	Jacqueline Banerjee
Sir Walter Scott	Harriet Harvey Wood
Olive Senior	Denise de Caires Narain
The Sensation Novel	Lyn Pykett
P. B. Shelley	Paul Hamilton
Sir Philip Sidney & his Circle	Martin Woodcock
Iain Sinclair	Robert Sheppard
Christopher Smart	Neil Curry
Charlotte Smith & Helen Williams	Angela Keane
Wole Soyinka	Mpalive Msiska
Muriel Spark	Brian Cheyette
Edmund Spenser	Colin Burrow
Gertrude Stein	Nicola Shaughnessy
Laurence Sterne	Manfred Pfister
Bram Stoker	Andrew Maunder
Graham Swift	Peter Widdowson
Jonathan Swift	Ian Higgins
Swinburne	Catherine Maxwell
Elizabeth Taylor	N. R. Reeve
Alfred Tennyson	Seamus Perry
W. M. Thackeray	Richard Salmon
D. M. Thomas	Bran Nicol
Three Lyric Poets	William Rowe

RECENT & FORTHCOMING TITLES

Title   Author

J. R. R. Tolkien	*Charles Moseley*
Leo Tolstoy	*John Bayley*
Charles Tomlinson	*Tim Clark*
Anthony Trollope	*Andrew Sanders*
Victorian Quest Romance	*Robert Fraser*
Marina Warner	*Laurence Coupe*
Edith Wharton	*Janet Beer*
Oscar Wilde	*Alexandra Warrick*
Angus Wilson	*Peter Conradi*
Mary Wollstonecraft	*Jane Moore*
Women's Gothic 2/e	*E. J. Clery*
Women Poets of the 19th Century	*Emma Mason*
Women Romantic Poets	*Anne Janowitz*
Women Writers of Children's Classics	*Mary Sebag-Montefiore*
Women Writers of the 17th Century	*Ramona Wray*
Virginia Woolf 2/e	*Laura Marcus*
Working Class Fiction	*Ian Haywood*
W. B. Yeats	*Edward Larrissy*
Charlotte Yonge	*Alethea Hayter*

TITLES IN PREPARATION

Title   Author

Ama Ata Aidoo	*Nana Wilson-Tagoe*
Martin Amis	*Nicholas Bentley*
James Baldwin	*Douglas Field*
Elizabeth Barrett Browning	*Simon Avery*
Black British Writers	*Deidre Osborne*
Charlotte Brontë	*Stevie Davies*
Basil Bunting	*Martin Stannard*
John Bunyan	*Tamsin Spargoe*
Margaret Cavendish	*Kate Lilly*
Bruce Chatwin	*Kerry Featherstone*
G.K. Chesterton	*M. Hurley*
Cymbeline	*Peter Swaab*
Charles Darwin	*Rick Rylance*
Janet Frame	*Claire Bazin*
Nadine Gordimer	*Lewis Nkosi*
Geoffrey Grigson	*R. M. Healey*
David Hare	*Jeremy Ridgman*
Bessie Head	*Dorothy Driver*
Ben Jonson	*Anthony Johnson*
Jack Kerouac	*Michael Hrebebiak*
Jamaica Kincaid	*Susheila Nasta*
Rosamond Lehmann	*Judy Simon*
George Meredith	*Jacqueline Banerjee*
Una Marson & Louise Bennett	*Alison Donnell*
Toni Morrison	*Rebecca Ferguson*
R. K. Narayan	*Nicolas Grene*
Ngugi wa Thiong'o	*Brendon Nicholls*
Religious Poets of the 17th Century	*Helen Wilcox*
Samuel Richardson	*David Deeming*
Michèle Roberts	*Edith Frampton*
Ruskin & Pre-Raphaelite Poetry	*Lindsay Smith*
Olive Schreiner	*Carolyn Burdett*
Sam Selvon	*Ramchand & Salick*
Charlotte Smith & Helen Williams	*Angela Keane*
R. L. Stevenson	*David Robb*
Tom Stoppard	*Nicholas Cadden*
David Storey	*George Hyde*
Dylan Thomas	*Chris Wiggington*
Three Avant Garde Poets	*Peter Middleton*
Twelfth Night	*Michael Dobson*
Victorian Sages	*Gavin Budge*
Derek Walcott	*Stephen Regan*
Evelyn Waugh	*Ann Pasternak Slater*
Women's Poetry at the Fin de Siècle	*Anna Vadillo*
William Wordsworth	*Nicola Trott*